101 WAYS
TO
GET GREAT PUBLICITY

Timothy R V Foster

This book is dedicated to my sister, Noni

Acknowledgements
I want to thank Michael Johnson and Michael Seymour for
their help in vetting this book and the many people mentioned
in the text who assisted me with input and suggestions.

First published in 1993

Kogan Page Limited
120 Pentonville Road
London N1 9JN

© Timothy R V Foster 1993

British Library Cataloguing in Publication Data

A CIP record for this book is available from the British Library.

ISBN 0–7494–0958–4 Pbk
ISBN 0–7494–1082–5 Hbk

Typeset by DP Photosetting, Aylesbury, Bucks
Printed and bound in Great Britain by
Clays Ltd, St Ives plc

Contents

Understanding the Basics about Publicity   **9**
1 Understand your objectives *10*
2 Understand your audiences *11*
3 Be strategic *13*
4 Understand the media *14*
5 Understand the value of third-party endorsement *16*
6 'Brainstorm' ideas *17*
7 Be relevant *18*
8 Know when irrelevance works *19*
9 Do some research *19*
10 Be an authority *21*
11 Know your journalists *21*
12 Know your message *25*
13 Test ideas *25*
14 Support claims with facts *26*
15 Demonstrate improvement *27*
16 Understand the value of negatives and positives *27*
17 Update your audiences *28*
18 Understand the angle of a story *28*
19 Know your context *31*
20 Take the initiative *31*
21 Don't lie *31*
22 Correct errors *32*
23 Track and refine results *33*
24 Run your programme or it will run you *34*

Improving Your Image   **35**
25 Be environmental *36*
26 Be educational *37*
27 Sponsor sports *38*
28 Sponsor the arts *39*
29 Save something from disaster/extinction *40*

30 Clean something up   *40*
31 Hold a race   *41*
32 Go for the impossible dream   *41*
33 Be known for doing good things   *42*
34 If you can't donate money, donate kind   *42*
35 Ask for money   *43*

Understanding the Basics of Media Relations   **44**
36 Produce a press kit   *44*
37 Issue a press release   *45*
38 Produce a backgrounder   *47*
39 Include a fact sheet   *50*
40 Use a Q & A sheet   *51*
41 Use a spokesperson   *52*
42 Use media training   *53*
43 Hold a press conference   *54*
44 Hold a photocall   *55*
45 Do video vox pops   *57*
46 Use a video news release   *58*
47 Use radio clips   *60*
48 Do a media tour   *61*
49 Hold a radio phone-in   *63*
50 Have a telephone hotline   *63*
51 Use 'advertorials'   *64*

Creating Your Own Media   **66**
52 Offer a brochure   *66*
53 Produce a newsletter   *67*
54 Produce a magazine   *68*
55 Write an article   *69*
56 Write a book   *71*
57 Distribute flyers or handbills   *72*
58 Make a film or video   *72*

Involving Others in Your Message   **75**
59 Understand stakeholders   *75*
60 Appeal to special interests   *76*
61 Involve a celebrity   *77*
62 Involve a charity   *78*
63 Involve a politician   *78*

64 Involve royalty *78*
65 Involve a sportsperson *79*
66 Involve an animal *80*
67 Create an advisory board *81*
68 Use allies *81*
69 Involve customers *82*
70 Involve suppliers *82*
71 Involve employees *82*
72 Involve the community *83*
73 Involve the family *83*
74 Get signatures *84*
75 Create a coalition of like-minded people *84*
76 Use ambassadors *85*
77 Involve an expert or specialist *85*

Designing Special Events   **87**
78 Hold a symposium or seminar *87*
79 Hold a screening *88*
80 Throw a party *88*
81 Hold a teleconference *88*
82 Hold a contest *90*
83 Give an award *90*
84 Buy up the house *93*
85 Have a booth where the crowds are *93*
86 Participate in a trade show or exhibition *94*
87 Have a 'total experience/activity' day *94*

Using Stunts to Get Ink   **96**
88 Design a stunt *96*
89 Build a house *97*
90 Hold a sit-in *97*
91 Get arrested *97*
92 Go on a hunger strike *98*

Dealing with Adverse Publicity   **99**
93 Know what causes adverse publicity *99*
94 Know the cost of doing nothing *100*
95 Realise that negative publicity festers *101*
96 Avoid adverse publicity *102*
97 Be prepared *102*

98   Simulate a crisis   *105*
99   Know the key steps in handling a crisis   *105*
100 Know what they want to know   *107*
101 Handling the news beyond the team   *108*

Index   **109**

Understanding the Basics about Publicity

Before we go too far in our exploration of ways to get great publicity, I think it will be helpful to review some basics.

Publicity is defined in my dictionary as any information, usually printed, which brings a person, place, thing or cause to the notice or attention of the public. Also, any procedure or act that seeks to gain this. *Roget's Thesaurus* comes up, under the heading of publicity, with limelight, spotlight, public eye, common knowledge.

In the context of this book, publicity is not the same thing as advertising, although advertising could be defined as above. What I mean by publicity is the task of bringing to the attention of defined target audiences a specific message by means *other* than paid advertising.

Paid advertising is the process of telling people about or praising a product or service through announcements in the media – newspapers, magazines, radio, television, cinemas, posters, neon signs, handbills, skywriting and so on. An advertisement is created and a medium is selected to carry the message. The advertiser pays for the use of the space or airtime, and the announcement appears as contracted. Most of the time, it is absolutely clear to the audience that what they are exposed to in this way is an advertisement. They can believe or not, depending on their predilections or tastes and the quality of the advertising.

In the commercial world, most advertising is created and placed by advertising agencies. The revenues from advertising enable the medium either to provide its service in its entirety (as with television or radio and some publications) or to reduce the cost of its subscription (as with newspapers or magazines). And, of course, advertising can be just a source of revenue to the medium, as with outdoor posters, hoardings or neon signs on the sides of buildings.

Publicity, while it may very well cost money, is not obtained through the overt exchange of funds for a message delivered by a medium. Rather, it is the generation of interest in a subject in such a way as to earn attention in its own right. It is the creation of 'face time' (measured in seconds of personal television exposure) and the 'sound bite' (the succinct few words that manage to get into a news item on radio or TV. The term 'publicity stunt' is used when the generation of interest is purely and simply to gain publicity for a cause. Suffragettes chaining themselves to railings are an example, as are people who go on hunger strikes.

Such publicity might cost nothing, as in the two examples above, or there might be fees paid to an agency or consultancy to come up with and execute ideas or a publicity pro-gramme. It might be the cost of sponsorship, or fees to speakers or performers, or donations to a charity, or the provision of sports uniforms with the sponsor's name printed on them.

In some cases, magazines will print an article (that you supply) in return for a fee, or in return for some paid advertising. They may or may not (usually they do not) identify the article as a 'paid' insertion.

So that's what I mean by publicity. This section is about the basics of these kinds of publicity.

Way 1 Understand your objectives

Being clear about what you want your publicity to achieve will go a long way towards helping you get the right kind of publicity. The best way to do this is to evolve and write down your objective – your aim or goal. It is not enough to say: 'To obtain publicity for the project' – it's too wishy-washy. You need to specify what the getting of the publicity is intended to do. You need to specify a *measurable* result.

For example, my publicity objective for this book is: 'To create great publicity for this book so that it is seen that it:

● Practises what it preaches

- Works
- Must be worth having if you are interested in getting great publicity

as measured by a broad cross-section of positive reviews and stories in the media, letters from readers and bulk purchases by interested parties.'

I suggest, in phrasing your objective statement, you always start with the word 'to', putting the statement in the infinitive. This adds impetus.

Note that, above, I said 'publicity objective'. You can have all kinds of objectives related to your project or activity. Don't get them confused. You might have a marketing objective:

- To achieve a 10 per cent share of the market within two years

For this book, my marketing objective is:

- To become the best-selling book in its subject area within one year.

You might have a communications objective:

- To increase awareness of the link between cigarette smoking and lung cancer.

For this book, my communications objective is: to demonstrate in a highly readable and actionable manner the best ways to get effective (= 'great') publicity.

It's not a bad idea to print the objective out in large letters and hang it on your wall where you will see it all the time. It will help to keep you focused.

Way 2   Understand your audiences

Who are you trying to reach with your publicity? There are many ways of thinking about this question. You can aim at the people who you want to take some direct action as a result of the knowledge gained, let's call them the users. You can aim at people that the users listen to. They are called 'opinion formers' if they are going to be *proactive* about your message, or 'influencers' if they're going to be more *reactive*. You can aim at allies of these people. The more specific you can be in identifying all these people, the easier it will be to design a programme for getting great publicity.

Once again, taking this book as an example, the audiences are:

- *Users*: potential readers of the book, defined as:
  - Small business managers/proprietors
  - Charities
  - Professional organisations and trade associations
  - Chambers of Commerce
  - Trade development boards
  - Travel/tourist boards
  - Independent consultants
  - Self-employed people
  - Public relations people
  - Public relations agencies/consultancies
  - Clients of these organisations
  - Freelances
  - Teachers
  - Students
  - Libraries
- *Opinion formers:* reviewers in the media that reach the above people, for example, media such as:
  - Print
    - Magazines
    - Newspapers
      Daily
      Weekly
  - Broadcast
    - Radio
    - TV
  in these subjects:
  - PR
  - Advertising
  - Marketing

- General business
- Book trade
● *Influencers:*
  - Department of Trade and Industry
  - Confederation of British Industry
  - Federation of Small Businesses
  - Training and Enterprise Councils

The idea of understanding your audience extends beyond identifying who they are to understanding what are good ways to communicate with them. Some people are very busy and pressed for time, such as doctors or top management of corporations. Messages aimed at them within the realm of their day-to-day activities get very little attention. If you write them a letter, you need to grab their interest in the first paragraph. But reaching these same people when they doff their working attire can be an entirely different proposition. Then you can get to them through their interests or hobbies or pet projects.

Way 3   Be strategic

Being strategic means considering the consequences of proposed actions and acting accordingly, rather than just flying off and doing something because it sounds like a good idea. It means assembling your thinking in a cohesive way and reviewing the possible interactions and side benefits of a group of activities, so that you can take advantage of synergies that might exist.

Chess is *the* game of strategy. You wouldn't make a chess move without looking at all the possible consequences, would you? Yet how many times have you found yourself responding to some impetus very quickly, feeling good about your fast action and suddenly discovering an opportunity growing out of it that hadn't even occurred to you, and by the time you discovered it, it's too late to take advantage of? So you need to be strategic.

My strategy for this book?

● Use every possible one of the 101 ways to great publicity in developing publicity for this book – make the book live by its own rules and become its own best example.

Way 4   Understand the media

The word media is the plural of the word medium. So you don't say the media *is*, you say the media *are*. What are the media? In publicity terms, they are collectively all the vehicles through which publicity can be channelled:

- Print
- Electronic
- Other

Print includes newspapers, magazines, journals, newsletters, books, brochures, pamphlets and mail.

Electronic media, often called *broadcast* media, include radio and television, and audio and videotapes. They also include telecom-based activities like phone-message lines, hot lines, faxes and such.

Other means all kinds of things that are none of the above, like speeches, events, meetings, exhibitions and so on.

Another way of looking at the media is the means by which they are received by their audiences. There is a contention, especially in the print area, that people are more likely to be influenced by media they pay for than by media they get free. In the world of magazines, there are plenty that are free, supported entirely by their advertisers. As well as many trade publications, we also have the freebies handed out to commuters on their way to work, and the lifestyle magazines that are distributed door to door. The magazines that come with the Sunday papers really fall in the same category, but, because they come with something you pay for, they probably carry a bit more credibility.

In the UK, television is funded by the annual licence (BBC), by advertising (commercial channels) and by subscription (most satellite channels). Because of the power of the medium, the above argument is less valid.

Media may be categorised in many other ways, such as by

frequency of issue (daily, weekly, monthly, etc), by geographical coverage (Tyne–Tees, Birmingham, national UK, Europe, etc), by type of audience (men interested in sports, aviation industry executives, psychiatrists, teenagers, etc), by content (lifestyle, cooking, fashion, personality, etc), by publisher (News International, Mirror Group, Haymarket Group, etc), by style (quality dailies, tabloids, in-flight magazines, etc). You can probably think of many other ways of grouping the media.

The use of electronic media is expanding. Now it is quite common for a *videocassette* to be distributed free to target audiences to carry a message (a method used extensively in the 1992 US presidential election campaign). Shareholders of a company can order a video of the annual general meeting. You can order a free *floppy disk* that gives you a comparision of new cars to run on your personal computer from at least one manufacturer. You can call a *premium-rate telephone number* and hear a recorded message, while paying perhaps 50p per minute for the privilege.

British Telecom recently introduced the Business Information Line, a *free 0800 number*, that gives you a 7½ minute recorded documentary about the importance of relationship marketing and how the telephone can be used in this area. It ends with another 0800 number to call if you want to order a booklet.

Faxback is an *automated fax response device* that you call from a touch-tone telephone. A recorded message quizzes you on what you want, asking you to press numbers on your phone to reply. In this way it determines which information to send you, and then 'zaps' it immediately to the fax machine of your choice. *Teletext* lets you receive hundreds of messages over your television set.

The 'other' category is also very interesting. This includes invitations to free seminars, free tickets to a trade show, 'dialogue' booths at high-traffic locations where you can talk to experts in an identified field of interest, and experience-type events, like being able to drive a Formula One sports car at Brands Hatch racetrack or attend a hot-air balloon party.

An innovative example is the Gatorade PGA (Professional Golf Association) European Tour Physiotherapy Unit. Gatorade is a thirst quencher, billed as the world's largest-selling sports refreshment. They want to be identified as a serious product used by pros. So they supplied a well-equipped mobile fitness unit installed in a large bus, which attended every event in the European tour. They had a physiotherapist on hand, as well as TV sets to monitor the tournament. Golfers were invited to relax with a cool drink and take advice on sports nutrition and rehydration, in a comfortable environment.

An important component of this type of activity is the media launch. This is where appropriate journalists and other members of the media are invited to a press conference to hear about the event and sample it. Then, hopefully, they will go away and write it up. Maybe a television producer will decide the bus is a good place to conduct some interviews with the players, thus getting the bus into the background on TV shots. Everything has to work together.

For a really helpful overview of the media, I recommend *The Media Guide*, edited by Steve Peak, a *Guardian* book published by Fourth Estate. It is updated every year and contains a vast array of valuable information for less than £10 (as I write).

Way 5 Understand the value of third-party endorsement

You must have seen that sign, found in many retail establishments. It goes something like this: 'If you like our service, please tell your friends. If you don't, please tell us.' It's an extremely good idea. It's based on the concept that word-of-mouth is one of the most powerful forms of communication. It's based on the idea of third-party endorsement. The old Packard car used a variation on the theme with its slogan, 'Ask the man who owns one.'

Which is more powerful: for me, the author, to tell you this is a really great book, or for a trusted friend or public figure to tell you? You *know*. Now what's important is for the endorser to be *relevant*. Who would you pay more attention to as an endorser of this book – footballer Paul Gascoigne (Gazza) or business troubleshooter Sir John Harvey–Jones?

Some of your best messengers can be your own customers or

users. Do you actively encourage this? You should! If you serve your customers well, they will be happy to spread a positive word. What an incentive to give good service!

In the world of generating publicity, the obtaining of authentic third-party endorsement rightfully enjoys a lot of effort – it's that important.

So who would be good endorsers for this book?

- Entrepreneurs?
  - Richard Branson (Virgin)
  - Alan Sugar (Amstrad)
- Gurus?
  - Sir John Harvey–Jones
- Professionals?
  - PR people
  - Advertising people
  - Marketing people
  - Media people

and who else?

How do you get them to provide an endorsement? Start by asking. In the case of this book, you'd send a copy of the proofs and invite them to read the book and make a comment. Some will, some won't. Obviously, if you can work this out through personal contact or a trusted introducer, so much the better. The introducer, in effect, becomes an interim third-party endorser.

You can carry out activities that generate third-party endorsement. In Hollywood, they have sneak previews of new films to gauge audience reaction and to develop a buzz. You could hold a private screening for influential people. What you want is to get (the right kind of) people talking about your project in positive terms.

Way 6   Brainstorm ideas

Once you have an idea of your objectives, of your audiences and you understand the need to be strategic, you may find it helpful to hold a brainstorming session to develop or fine-tune your strategy, or to come up with some tactics based on your strategy.

A brainstorming session will help you to generate a lot of ideas quickly. It's based on the premise that a group of people working together, under good direction, can evolve a wider variety of ideas and possibilities than those same people working as individuals. These sessions can be a lot of fun.

The advantages of brainstorming come from there being a lower level of inhibition within the group compared with a more formal meeting, and a higher level of enthusiasm. Individual competitiveness needs to be managed so that it doesn't create barriers caused by one person trying to top another all the time.

Brainstorming sessions require an experienced facilitator to direct and control them. The facilitator's role is *not* to make up ideas, but to assist the participants in evolving them.

Don't have too many people in the session (a maximum of eight, plus the facilitator and maybe a scribe to record everything on flip charts, is a good guideline). Don't run it for too short a time (you need at least three to four hours to do a good job).

Way 7   Be relevant

My dictionary defines relevant as 'bearing upon or relating to the matter at hand, pertinent, to the point'. As you evaluate your ideas for getting great publicity, relevance is an important criterion. Will your idea help the cause?

Being relevant means helping things to move in the direction of the desired result. There is a tendency in some quarters, for example, to use sex as a means of getting attention. In fact, you must have seen the ad headlined simply with the word 'SEX', followed by a sub-head that says something like, '**Now that we have your attention**, *have you considered the advantages of linked investment trusts?'*

The American feminist magazine *MS* used to run a column called *'No Comment'*. This ran examples of blatantly sexist advertising or editorial, and was a good lesson in the importance of relevance.

Being relevant means, for example, using a spokesperson

who has some link with the message. In 1990, Cadbury's Chocolate Break, a hot drink, carried out a programme called Swimathon, involving people doing targeted swims to raise money for charity. The spokesman was Duncan Goodhew, the Olympic gold medal swimmer. He swam and spoke at the launch held at Windsor Safari Park. What's the relevance here? Easy, the photo opportunity was Duncan swimming with the dolphins in their dolphinarium!) He was linked to the programme through posters and other appearances.

What's relevant for this book? Activities relating to business, to publicity, to the media – in fact anything, because even something totally irrelevant could work, since it's an example of how *not* to achieve a result, as described in this book!

Way 8   Know when irrelevance works

Irrelevance can work, as above, but note that it was made relevant. Can you be totally irrelevant and still benefit from it? Yes. What about all those charity runs? Crossing the Antarctic on foot to raise money for multiple sclerosis research is totally irrelevant, I would venture. But it is the sort of event that gets good media coverage, so it can raise the profile of MS as a terrible disease, with no known cure, that needs financial help.

Way 9   Do some research

One of the best ways to get publicity is to do some research and then publish the findings. Newspapers love headlines like:

80% of 12-year-olds can't spell aquarium

Here's an exercise. Take today's newspaper and go through it looking for stories that are driven by research. Here's what I found in *The Times* today.

● **High street sales fall in October**
(The latest survey from the Confederation of British Industry shows...)

- **EC jobless up**
  (According to Eurostat, the EC statistics office...)

- **Private consultants are relying on public sector work to stay afloat in recession**
  (In its latest survey of chief executives, the Management Consultancies Association...)

- **Crisis? What crisis?**
  (According to a recent Gallup poll, over two thirds of middle-aged men believe the mid-life...)

Charles Russam heads an organisation called GMS Consultancy. This is a business that maintains a database of independent consultants and seeks to find work for them, a sort of temporary-help bureau for managers. For the last two years, GMS has produced a research report entitled *The GMS Annual Survey – The Independent Consultancy Market*. This is a 56-page A4 booklet containing all kinds of data on independent consultants. The amount of 'ink' this has earned is huge – half pages in *The Times* and *The Sunday Times*, stories in *The Financial Times* and so on. The research went a long way to positioning GMS as a serious contender in the 'interim management' business.

If you want a headline about what you want to promote, what is the research *you* have to do to generate it?

To promote this book, I might want a headline that says something like:

72% of small business owners believe they frequently miss out on publicity opportunities

Now what's the research I have to do to drive that headline (given that we'd use the actual percentage, rather than the made-up figure in the example)?

Somehow I should do a survey of small business owners to find out their attitudes towards publicity. One of the questions might be:

- Do you feel you never/sometimes/frequently miss out on publicity opportunities?

Way 10 Be an authority

An authority is the person the media turn to when they need an opinion or a comment about something. If you watch UK television news regularly, you'll keep seeing the same faces in connection with certain types of stories. Whenever there's a major air crash or a question of airline safety, there's David Learmount, Air Transport Editor of *Flight International*. If the question is about military aircraft, there's Paul Beaver, Editor of *Jane's Defence Weekly*. The business news is always loaded with this fleet of economists and analysts from the various brokers and banks. For small business, it's Steve Alambritis of the Federation of Small Businesses. If the subject is prostitution, there's Miss Whiplash.

A good way to become an authority, if you're not already the editor of a relevant publication, is to write a book on the subject. Being the author of an appropriate book confers a mantle of expertise on you (see Way 56). Or you could be the head of or spokesman for a trade association.

Of what could you be the authority?

Way 11 Know your journalists

My dictionary defines journalism as the work of gathering news for, writing for, editing or directing the publication of a newspaper or other periodical. I will add to that 'or other medium', eg, TV or radio. So where do they gather their news? They can hardly read the newspaper for it! They have to write what goes *into* the newspaper.

So crime reporters monitor the police radio channels with their scanners and sit in courtrooms. Maybe they rely on informants or friendly policemen at 'headquarters'. Sports reporters go to football games or cricket matches or polo games and report on what happened. They interview the players and the coaches and maybe some of the fans. And they put together a story. Political reporters hang around Parliament, Whitehall or Capitol Hill. They call their friends who may be 'usually reliable sources' to confirm or deny rumours. Gardening reporters go to flower shows and talk to expert horticulturalists, or they look at their diaries and suggest it's time to lay the compost.

What about the journalists who write about what you do? If you run a company that builds engines for Jaguars, how do you suppose the journalists who cover that area get their information? What about those who write about computers? Or about food manufacturing?

The answer is they get a lot of their information from people who want something to be known. They crave information. Give it to them!

I want people to know about this book. So I should talk to business journalists, especially those who cover small business, book reviewers and people who cover the book trade. I should also talk to journalists who work in the PR/advertising/marketing field.

Good journalists aim to present a balanced point of view. They will often disagree with a person in an interview just to reflect the other side. You'll see this a lot in political interviews on TV. A while ago, I developed a seminar based on my first book in the 101 Ways series – *101 Ways to Succeed as an Independent Consultant*. The seminar was called 'How to Market Yourself as an Independent Consultant'. I was interviewed by a reporter at *PR Week*. He said: 'You're just doing this to sell more books aren't you?' 'Well, the seminar costs £120 and the books costs about £6, so it would be more likely the other way around,' I said. So when the article appeared, there was the story, accompanied by my photograph. The caption? 'Foster. Denies book tie in'.

Some journalists are well known for holding strong opinions, which may be reflected in a column they write. They may be way out of balance.

Journalists may take the position that they have a duty to inform the police. In the USA, you have freedom of the press constitutionally guaranteed. And you have the Freedom of Information Act which prohibits withholding unclassified information and ensures that citizens have the right of access. In the UK, on the other hand, you have no such thing. You have 'gag orders' and 'reporting restrictions' and the Official Secrets Act.

About four years ago I wanted to find out how many licensed civilian private pilots there were in the UK, so I called the Civil Aviation Authority. I got through to the right person, and posed the question. 'Who are you?' he said. I gave him my name. 'Who are you with?' 'Just me,' I said. 'Why do you want to know?' It went on in this vein for a few minutes. Total suspicion as to my motives and at the end of it all he couldn't answer the question because they don't know!

Anyway, the point of all this is that you should get to know the journalists in your field. Go through the trade magazines. Make a list of the people at each magazine who could be important to you. Then think of a reason to talk to them and call them up. Introduce yourself. Tell them what areas you are involved with and offer to be a source of information. Be accessible and helpful and you'll be the one they call when they want to get an opinion or to verify an industry fact.

What turns a journalist on? An exclusive! What used to be called a scoop. But remember, the hot news you have to offer may well be considered only mildly interesting by someone not directly involved when compared with the other news pouring in all the time. Your story has to make it against huge competition.

Think of it this way: all day long, journalists must choose from the continuous flow of data received (from other reporters, from press agencies all over the world, through press conferences, press releases or just people like you phoning them up). They must ask: 'Of all this *stuff*, what is the top story I can run, given time and space limitations?'

The time limitation is the deadline, which is sacred. This is the moment after which it's too late – unless, of course, someone yells 'Hold the front page!' So when you are talking to a journalist, bear in mind that they need to complete the story by a certain moment, and they may suddenly become busy on other things as that deadline approaches.

Another factor to recognise is that the journalist you speak to may very well not be the last person to touch the copy. They have editors and sub-editors, whose role in life it is to keep everything tight. That's why whole chunks of stories will suddenly disappear from the final version.

What is the journalist looking for?

● A story that will interest the medium's key audiences

- An unusual or provocative angle
- Ability to meet the deadline
- Accuracy, verified facts

Don't forget, journalists often have a hidden agenda. They are always looking for a means to build their careers. Does what you have move them in the direction of career advancement, regression, or is it just neutral and blah?

It's a good idea to keep a log of your journalist contacts so you can get hold of them quickly when you need to and you can be immediately up to date on the conversations you have had in the past. Here's a format to help you do that.

Journalists contact log

Publication	Contact name Title	
Telephone	Fax	
Story interests	Personal notes	
Date	**Contact notes**	**Action**

Way 12   Know your message

Being clear about your message is a primary requirement of getting great publicity. Your message is what you want your audience to take away – the sentiment they would play back when reflecting on your delivery of the message. It's what you would want them to say to a friend when telling them about it.

How do you get to the message? You could start by asking the question: 'What do I want my target audience to think when they think about this product/service/etc?' Ideally, the message should have a benefit stated in it.

In *101 Ways to Succeed as an Independent Consultant* – I gave my secret for recognising a benefit from a feature, and for getting to the *ultimate benefit*. The ultimate benefit is the most compelling one, based on that specific feature. I repeat it here.

My secret is based on the word *so*. All you do is make a statement about the product or service, and then say 'so...?' There needs to be a slight questioning inflection in your voice. And you keep saying 'so...?' until you get to the ultimate benefit.

For example: 'This video recorder (VCR) has its own tuner, so...? You can record a programme on one channel while you are watching one on another channel, so...? You can run your life on your own terms, not on the dictates of a programme schedule, so...? You can get more out of your time, and do what you want when you want, so...? You can be free, so...?' When you run out of responses to the word 'so', you should be at the ultimate benefit.

A good way of getting the message right is to hold a brainstorming session to develop it (see Way 6).

Way 13   Test ideas

It doesn't matter how brilliant you and your team are. You may come up with what seems like the most incredible scheme to get publicity, roll it out and watch it go nowhere.

What you need to do is to check it out in advance. Check with experienced people, check with a few members of the target audience, check with your client, check with the retailers. You may need to disguise the concept slightly in order not to give the game away. You also don't want to build in bias for or against the idea by revealing the client or message sender.

If you are offering something by mail, you can do test mailings. If you are devising some grand and complex event, you could hold a focus-group session. This is where you get groups of people together in a controlled environment and conduct an in-depth enquiry into your idea. This process is quite expensive, compared to making a few phone calls or sending out questionnaires, but if it is done properly it's well worth while.

You can use a focus group to identify perceived problems with your approach. You can show them parts of your concept, or a write-up of the service, or a mock-up of the product. Skilfully handled, you can get a lot of information and a better understanding of your audience very quickly. By holding several focus groups with different types of people: heavy users, light users, non-users, men, women, doctors, airline pilots, mothers, mothers with teenage daughters, teenagers, etc, you can *focus* on the information you need to develop. You can also conduct them regionally: north, south, urban, rural, seaside, inland, Spanish, Italian, multinational, and so on.

Way 14   Support claims with facts

Any claims you make should be supported by some evidence of the validity of those claims. The weaker the support the less powerful the claim. Consider these two sentences:

1. It is believed that many people travelling more than 50 miles to work on commuter trains have to stand for most of their journey.
2. According to a survey conducted by the Allied Passengers Association last January, 60 per cent of commuters travelling more than 50 miles to work on trains have to stand for at least half of their journey.

When you are quoting facts, also quote the source and date of those facts. This might be from research you have conducted, or from other research that already exists (often known as *desk* research). If you use desk research, you may have to get permission to cite the information, although this is usually a formality.

Your support may also be a quote from a person: 'According to Manfred Hertzbach, 54, director general of the association, unless the deficit is overcome by 31 March, the ballet company will have to close immediately thereafter.' (I don't know why they always put people's ages in – I suppose it's to distinguish this Manfred Hertzbach from Manfred Hertzbach, 23, the well-known bungee jumper.)

Way 15   Demonstrate improvement

One way of getting a good headline is to show that some improvement has taken place (these are made-up examples):

98 per cent of directory enquiries calls answered within two rings

Car fatalities decrease by 39 per cent since mandatory seat-belt use introduced

Supermarket check-out lines move faster thanks to scanners

Any claim of improvement needs to be supported by some verifiable source (see Way 14).

Way 16   Understand the value of negatives and positives

When something negative needs to be addressed, there are two ways of talking about it, the negative way and the positive way – is the glass half empty or half full?

Even if you are trying to kill something someone else is doing, a positive benefit can be used. You can cite the negatives first: 'If this airline merger is allowed to take place, it will result in the loss of 1400 jobs.' And you can end up with a positive: 'the alternative will result in greater choice and flexibility for passengers.'

Everything can be stated negatively and positively. The negative inflicts or threatens pain, the positive, pleasure. People tend to avoid pain and seek out pleasure. Both are potent driving forces, especially when used in combination. Knowing what your ultimate message is will help you to control the pros and cons of its delivery.

You want to make your message part of the solution, not part of the problem. Actions that are part of the solution always move in the direction of overcoming the problem. Actions that are part of the problem constantly delay or prevent arrival at the solution.

'Solution people' tend to be optimists and 'problem people' tend to be pessimists. Each can be detected by almost everything they say. 'We're running out of petrol,' is part of the problem. 'We'd better stop and get more petrol,' is part of the solution. 'I'm sorry that's out of stock,' is part of the problem. 'We'll have some more in on Tuesday,' is part of the solution.

Way 17   Update your audiences

One communication isn't enough. You have to keep plugging away. Every new communication should advance your story a little bit, giving a new insight or dimension to your message. It is, of course, important that you date every communication, because otherwise who is to know which version will eventually find its way into use?

Updates can be based on new or revised information, reactions to earlier communications, additional comments or speeches made, new results of test activities, revised time-tables – you name it.

Way 18   Understand the angle of a story

You can tell the same story several times over to different audiences if you understand the concept of the *angle* or *slant* of the story. It goes back to knowing what the medium is looking for in communicating to its audiences.

There are two broad categories of business publications, horizontal and vertical:

- Horizontal – those that cover several industries, perhaps from one point of view, eg:
  - *Marketing*
  - *Financial Times*
  - *The Economist*
  - *First Voice for Business*
  - *Home Run*
- Vertical – titles about the same industry, eg:
  - *Television Week*
  - *TV Producer*
  - *Broadcast*

Say you want to publicise this book. The story aimed at readers of a trade magazine such as *The Bookseller* would be about the book's marketing, and would discuss how the book fits in with other titles in the category – business books. The story aimed at readers of *PR Week* would talk about the author's experience in PR and give information about the book's content and, what it is intended to do. The story for the 'Your Own Business' column in *The Times, First Voice for Business* or *Home Run* would talk about how small businesses and independent people may have had trouble getting publicity and now there's a new book aimed at helping them overcome this barrier.

If you want to aim a story at several different publications in one vertical category, you need to come up with a different angle for each. There's a worksheet overleaf to help you do that. I've filled it in a bit to show its use.

1. Write in the broad subject of the story at the top.
2. There are three columns headed 'Title 1/Contact', 'Title 2/ Contact', etc.
3. In the first row marked 'Category', write in publication category under that heading, eg, Electronic media publications.
4. Then write in the title of each publication and your contact's name in each of the title boxes.
5. In the next row, marked 'Story angle', write in the angle you will use for each publication in the appropriate boxes.
6. If there are more than three titles in a category, use a larger format with more columns, or start a new row.

Story angle planner

Subject: *New VCR from Client Electronics PLC*

Publication	Title 1/ Contact	Title 2/ Contact	Title 3/ Contact
Category *Electronic media publications*	*Broadcasting* *J Doe Editor*	*Video Production* *R Roe Editor*	*Television Month* *A N Other Editor*
Story angle	*Use of VCRs in broadcast production*	*Use of VCRs in non-broadcast production*	*Use of VCRs in all education*
Category			
Story angle			
Category			
Story angle			

Way 19   Know your context

It is important to present your message in the right context. You need to recognise what's going on around you and make the story relevant to reality. In fact, the reality of the world around you may very well be the impetus for the story.

For example, a story about this book that reflects the marketplace context might have language like this in it:

> With the increasing tendency in the UK for people to be running their own businesses, there is a growing need for these people, often former managers within large organisations, to develop basic marketing – communications skills. One such skill is the art of generating publicity to promote a product, service or idea. In his new book, *101 Ways to Get Great Publicity*, author Timothy R V Foster, outlines ...

Way 20   Take the initiative

Being proactive is more conducive to getting the results you want than being reactive. If you're proactive, you have more control over the content of the message as well as where, how and to whom it is delivered.

This is particularly true if you are dealing with problems, as in a crisis. Large organisations increasingly plan for possible crises by developing preparedness programmes that spell out who does what, who says what and on what basis communications take place (see Way 97). This is so much more intelligent than sitting there with egg on your face saying, 'Wha?' when the reporter calls to ask why your company is killing babies or poisoning farm animals or whatever spin they put to it.

Way 21   Don't lie

If you tell the truth, you don't have to remember what you said. And you won't be challenged when, inevitably, the whole truth comes to light.

The biggest evidence I've seen of lying is in things like

performance specifications. I used to be involved in the aero-plane business, and did a brochure for a new Canadian light aircraft (long since defunct). We said the aircraft cruised at 125 mph, which was true. The president simply changed the cruising speed figures because they were too low! He insisted on putting 135 mph in the brochure. However, he missed the point that when journalists write up their 'pilot reports' in the aviation magazines, the first thing they do is try out the speeds. Thus they came up with lines like, 'We set the aircraft up for cruising speed at 6,000 feet, but we were only able to get 125 mph, vs. the 135 mph it quotes in the brochure. We were able to get 135 mph in a shallow dive, but the ground was approaching too fast for this to be a solution.' What do you suppose that kind of report did for the aircraft company's credibility?

It all goes back to Way 14 (Support claims with facts), with a little bit of Way 5 (Understand the value of third-party endorsement) thrown in. Surely an independent third party would not lie!

Way 22   Correct errors

To err is human. It's not whether you make a mistake that's the critical issue. It's how you handle it. If you deal with it promptly and honestly, it will not be held against you. But if you deny everything and try to bluster your way out of it, you'll get what you deserve.

I was at the International Air Tattoo at Fairford, Gloucester-shire directing a video for Japanese television. We were coordinating production through the press office. In the process, we were handed a press release. There was a glaring error in the headline. I pointed this out to the PRO. 'Oh, I'm *far* too busy to waste my time proofreading *press releases*,' she said. If you are press relations officer, what could be more impor-tant than an accurate press release?

This brings me to what I call the Declaration of Apathetic Commitment, which is: 'The job is not done until you have come up with a really good excuse as to *why* the job is not done!

Way 23 Track and refine results

What good is publicity if it doesn't work? They say any publicity is good publicity (as long as they spell the name right). But measuring the results is much more than an accuracy check. How do you measure results of publicity?

The most obvious initial step is to simply count the take-up of the story. Capture press clippings and videos of TV coverage. When I was head of advertising at the giant investment firm, Merrill Lynch, in New York, we conducted a major event called National Investment Seminar Week in 1976. In this, we held an investment seminar in each of our 450 offices all through the USA in the same week; 100,000 people attended throughout the country. Burson-Marsteller was hired to develop the public relations activity for this and all our other customer-relations programmes. It was the start of a long and important relationship for me.

After the 'Week' was over, Burson presented me with a book of press clippings as thick as a Manhattan telephone directory (about 8 cm). They estimated that the value of this publicity, if it had been purchased in the form of advertising, exceeded $5 million. We got incredible coverage, full pages of stories and photographs in local newspapers galore, quotes from speeches, interviews with our people. The programme later won the Silver Anvil Award of the Public Relations Society of America as the best marketing programme of the year (See Way 83).

Throughout the development activity, which ran ten months, we met regularly to determine what was happening. We wanted to make the event a bonanza, and our strategy included constant refinement of our actions. In this way we were able to take advantage of opportunities as they surfaced as a result of our initial steps, growing on developments that arose from what we were doing.

When astronauts fly to the moon, they don't just point the rocket at the moon and wait until they get there. They constantly measure and check, refining their routing all the time. Hence the phrase 'mid-course correction'. Better to do this *en route* than to find out at the last minute you're going to miss it!

So check what's going on all the time. Refine, refine, refine. Talk to people about what they are getting from your activity. Is the message coming through?

Way 24   Run your programme or it will run you

You have to seize control. No doubt you have some competitors. They don't work in a vacuum. Do you know what they are doing? Do they know what you are doing? Are they reacting to you or are you reacting to them? Who's in charge here?

If you followed the concepts outlined in this first chapter, you'll be a long way towards running your programme, so you will get the results you want, rather than what just happens.

Improving your Image

Your image, or that of your product, cannot be purchased. You have to get it the old-fashioned way. You have to *earn* it. Some people might refer to your image as goodwill or perhaps brand equity. Whatever you call it, I mean that intangible value that you own, that people respect when they think of you, your products or your services. Your image is very valuable. But it's hard to measure it in financial terms.

One way to build your image is to do good things. Especially do good things that the people you count as your customers or their influencers will appreciate as good things. And don't do bad things. Things that may not seem like bad things to you, but that might to your customer. It's not the reality of your actions, it's the *perception* by the audience that is the reality. In this area, the only thing that counts is what people think.

Nowadays people are immensely well informed about almost everything, to the extent that even the purchase of a bar of soap is a considered purchase, rather than an impulse buy. Look at some of the things that might go into a buyer's decision:

I want to wash my face. Here is a bar of soap. Before I buy it, let me ponder these questions about the makers:

- Do they test this soap on animals?
- Do they use recycled paper in their packaging?
- Do they pour chemicals into the waterways near their factory?
- Do they trade with countries that inhibit personal freedom?
- Do they use artificial colours?
- Is the fragrance excessive?

- Do they use animal fats in their production?
- Do they spend large amounts on TV advertising that I hate?
- Do they have good employer practices?
- Does their stock trade at a good price?
- Does their company have a good dividend record?
- Is their management beyond reproach?
- Do they sell their goods through stores that trade on Sundays?
- Is the company a good citizen?
- Do they treat women employees well (do they have senior executives who are women, do they provide daycare centres, do they give decent maternity leave, are their pay practices fair, etc)?
- Do they support the arts, sports, education?

You can see from the above considerations that selling a bar of soap these days involves all sorts of communication needs to convey the requisite information that will address the concerns of consumers. How does this apply to what you do?

Way 25 Be environmental

Green is *the* colour these days. Your environmental stance is an essential part of your image. Apple Computer now ships its products in brown cardboard boxes instead of the white ones it used in the past. The box comes with an explanation citing the environmental reasons for this. The rechargeable battery of the PowerBook on which this very tome is being written has instructions to return the dead unit to your dealer so that it can be disposed of safely, since it contains materials that are hazardous to the environment. My new chequebook from National Westminster Bank has the following statement on the inside: 'Cover printed on 60% recycled paper (30% wood-free unprinted waste, 30% woodfree printed waste) 40% virgin pulp.' How many other products do you see these days that have some kind of environmental message on them?

What this means is that environmentalism is a good hook for

your publicity activity. So a question you should ask whenever designing a publicity programme is: 'Is there an environmental angle here?' However, don't pick an environmental theme just because it's fashionable. The link must be real, or the story will be seen to be phony, which is more damaging than ignoring the environmental issues in the first place.

Way 26   Be educational

Educational programmes are an excellent way of building a constituency for your message over the long term. They are particularly effective in conveying information about health-care-related activities. For example, they could provide data on diseases such as asthma, or health risks such as excessive cholesterol. Straight advertising to the public of ethical drugs – those that may only be sold on prescription – is restricted by law, so often an educational approach presents a good solution to the producer's need to get information out to its end-users and influencers.

An educational programme can be aimed at children or at the general public. It is a way of conveying your message without an aura of hard sell. You are there to supply the information, and it is up to the audiences to draw what conclusions they may from your activity.

Our children are the future. If you want to start them off thinking good things about what you do, an educational programme can be the answer. This can also have an effect on their parents – positive or negative, depending on how well it's done.

The sorts of activities in this kind of programme include straight information delivery through conventional means such as booklets, videos, posters, lectures, as well as more interactive ideas such as games or collecting campaigns. An example might be a message about the value of your product or service, followed by an offer to do something helpful in return for the collection of proofs of purchase. The aluminium industry has made educational presentations on the merits of aluminium soft-drink cans, and they invite the children to collect empty cans for recycling. They then offer to make a donation to the school's gymnasium or science lab or whatever for each kilo of cans turned in.

By following this up with a story in the local paper, supported by pictures of the children standing on a huge mound of cans, they take advantage of the publicity opportunity. See how this works on so many levels:

● It teaches kids – the present and future consumers – about the product
● It gets the kids involved with boosting the sale of the product
● It helps the school, so they are happy to be involved
● It provides a nice angle to develop stories which put the sponsor in a good light in the media.

Way 27   Sponsor sports

Sports sponsorship provides an excellent way of involving the public in your story.

The sponsorship could range from advertising in the event's programmes, to providing uniforms for the team (suitably branded, of course), to signs around the playing field or arena, to full involvement so that the event is named after the sponsor, eg, the Seagram's Grand National, the Dunhill Cup and so on.

The way to select a sport for sponsorship is to ask these questions:

● Who do I want to reach with my message?
● What sporting events are these people attracted to?

If you sell lager, for instance, you'll probably want to reach young men aged 18–25. What sports are they interested in? How about football? If you sell an upmarket product aimed at fairly conservative individuals, you might sponsor golf. Hence Volvo sponsors the European PGA Tour. People interested in golf will thus tend to think good things about Volvo, which is exactly what they want.

An excellent source of further information on sponsorship

is the book *How to Get Sponsorship*, by Stuart Turner (Kogan Page).

Way 28   Sponsor the arts

The same rules apply as with sports. What realm of the arts does your audience love? If you are Pioneer stereos, you want to reach young people, teens and up. So you might sponsor the Madonna tour. An upmarket bank might sponsor an exhibition at the Royal Academy.

The benefits of sponsorship include being able to hold special events for key members of your target audience related to the activity you are sponsoring. For example, it might be an opening night cocktail party where your guests mingle with the stars of the show or an evening where they enjoy a sneak preview of the exhibit and such. There's a lot to be said for enabling your key clients to enjoy an exclusive relationship with the event.

Have you ever been to the Farnborough Air Show? Notice all those 'chalets' in multiple rows on the hill overlooking the airfield? Each chalet (there are hundreds of them) is hired by one of the exhibitors to provide high-level wining and dining for their customers and friends. Go inside (by invitation only) and enjoy a buffet lunch, drinks, an excellent view of the flying display, and the opportunity for some quiet chat about the benefits of the sponsor's new hydraulic landing-gear retraction system.

There's a nifty way of sponsoring the arts that may give you all the benefits of sponsorship without a great financial outlay, although there is a risk involved. It's sponsorship by guarantee. The entity that's seeking sponsorship, say a ballet company, establishes a budget for their event. If they sell enough seats, they'll earn a profit. If they don't they'll suffer a loss. The guarantor/sponsor simply undertakes to cover any loss, up to an agreed limit, should it occur. So merely by going at risk for, say £100,000, a sponsor can be seen to be endowing the particular art without actually laying out any vast amounts of cash. It might end up costing nothing, £10,000 or – horrors! – the full whack.

Way 29   Save something from disaster/ extinction

Being a saviour can work wonders for your image. The sorts of thing that can be saved are usually traditional historic institutions, such as a zoo, a symphony orchestra, a hospital, a library, a museum, a church, a school or maybe a historical building. Tesco supermarkets recently saved the historic art deco Hoover factory building in London by converting it internally to a food store, while preserving the wonderful exterior and gardens. Sir Terence Conran saved the Michelin Building in South Kensington by turning it into a restaurant named after the Michelin man, Bibendum.

Make sure you save what you want to save. In the sixties, London Bridge was saved from the rubbish dump by the developers of a new town in Arizona, Lake Havasu City, just south of Needles, California. They built an artificial lake to accommodate the old bridge, which was already destined to be replaced by a larger span in London. So as the old bridge was taken apart, each brick and stone was carefully numbered and coded so that it could all be put back together again Stateside. One small problem... the bridge they thought they were going to get was that neat double-decker we know as Tower Bridge. Imagine the surprise when they put together this giant granite Lego set and found it was just a fairly ordinary road bridge! Well at least it was famous in song.

Way 30   Clean something up

If your product has links with the world of detergents or cleaning, or you want to give work to a lot of Boy Scouts, you could get some neat publicity by doing a public-spirited clean-up of statues and major buildings, what with all the graffiti one sees. That's what Scotch-Brite, a cleaning pad made by 3M, did. Think of the photo opportunity, maybe a close-up of a statue with one of your workers straddling it in some peculiar way, scrubbing bird lime off the giant nose of some deceased notable.

The clean-up could also be seen as a good gesture in the

community – the sort of thing a good corporate citizen does, an example to us all.

Way 31 Hold a race

People are naturally competitive, so holding some kind of race will attract participants and, of course, publicity. The more off-beat the race, the better the story.

Many of the great moments in the history of flight were the result of sponsorship prizes. Louis Bleriot was the first to fly across the English Channel in 1909, thanks to a prize of £1000 offered by the *Daily Mail*. The same paper had earlier offered an identical prize for the first Briton to cover a mile in a British aeroplane, and later awarded £10,000 for the first non-stop crossing of the Atlantic (Alcock and Brown won that in 1919). Fast-forward to 1977 and we have Bryan Allen winning the Kremer prize of £50,000 for the first man-powered flight of a figure of eight over two pylons a half mile apart, which he did in the *Gossamer Condor*.

How about a race to the top of a skyscraper? How about the Glasgow Marathon? Or the London-to-Brighton bicycle race, sponsored by Flora margarine? And of course, there is the inevitable 'link to charity', where the participants get their friends to sponsor them for completing the race for so much a mile.

Way 32 Go for the impossible dream

Challenging people to go for the impossible dream has led to such results as Roger Bannister running the mile in under four minutes, Edmund Hillary climbing Mount Everest, Richard Branson and Per Lindstrand crossing the Atlantic in a hot-air balloon, Dick Rutan and Jeanna Yeager flying around the world non-stop without refuelling, and even Neil Armstrong walking on the moon! Landing a man on the moon was the ultimate example of image building, creating unparalleled recognition for American know-how, skill and courage, that did a lot to help US citizens feel closer together and to cause people around the world to gaze with awe at the accomplishment.

Way 33　Be known for doing good things

It's not enough just to be Mr Nice Guy and support all these public-spirited activities – you're trying to build your image, remember? A key part of doing good things, then, is to be recognised for it. That's what publicity is about. Unless anonymity is your objective, you want it to be known that the Scout troop is sponsored by your car dealership or whatever, so this means having a Scouting display in the showrooms, Scout livery on your courtesy cars, and Boy Scouts doing free car washes on your forecourt (it helps to bring in the customers).

Maybe you should even run a 'slogo' (my word for the 'slogan by the logo') in your advertising and on your letterheads. Hence you will see lines like '*Time Magazine*, world sponsors of the Olympic Games', or 'Gatorade, the official thirst quencher of the PGA Tour of Europe'.

Way 34　If you can't donate money, donate kind

Merrill Lynch is a global company, with a huge network of 24-hour dedicated telephone lines linking their offices. Every Christmas they open up their trading desks in places like London and New York to members of the local community to make free phone calls to their loved ones all over the world. And they get good coverage on the evening TV news in return, which is both publicity and image-enhancement. You can't buy that sort of coverage. You can only earn it. Note that a major aspect of the image business was fairly low-key, being aimed at the communities in which they are located.

The Corporate Angel Network consists of 525 corporations who make empty seats in their private corporate aircraft available free to cancer patients and their companions for transportation to specialised treatment centres around the world.

A major public relations agency donates its services (called 'pro bono' work) to Business in the Community, an organisation dedicated to improving corporate citizenship in Britain – an excellent example of corporate citizenship.

British Airways donated a 747 trip to over 200 terminally ill children to give them a visit to Disney World in Florida. *Project Dreamflight* was conceived by BA employees, and they donated their time to the project. Many sponsors gave incredible prizes (like a new Fiat and a Concorde round-the-world trip for two) in connection with a fund-raising campaign (I wrote and directed the fund-appeal video, which starred George Cole, who in turn gave his services). A further result was a documentary TV show reporting on the trip, shown on UK network TV a few months later.

McDonald's gave free food all day to the firefighters at the Windsor Castle fire, resulting in the immortal line 'What's a Big Mac?' from one of the royal princes as he was handed one by a begrimed fireman, all widely reported, of course.

Apple Computer donated Macintoshes, printers and software to the committee for the Manchester Olympic bid. And so on, and so on. What have you got or can you do that will help others, and help improve your image as well?

Way 35   Ask for money

Poppy day (November 11) is an example of how to improve your image by asking for money. Is there any self-respecting personality who would permit face time on TV without a poppy in the lapel in early November? Prince Charles was wearing one in *South Korea*! So part of the image strengthening comes from the poppy-sales boxes located at the receptionists of the many supporting organisations in the run up to Remembrance Day. We sell poppies, so we must be good citizens.

This extends to fountains in Holiday Inns loaded down with submerged coins, supported by a sign saying something like: 'All coins thrown in here are donated to the St Catherine's Hospice'.

And then there are the charity dinner dances, with the inevitable tombola. The sponsor that organises the event is creating a good image, while raising money for a deserving cause.

Yes, asking for money can be good for you.

Understanding the Basics of Media Relations

This section is about the tools and techniques of the trade. These are what you employ to establish, build and maintain your relations with the media. We'll talk about press materials, such as press releases and press kits, press conferences, photo-calls, video news releases, media tours and the like – the basic stuff. And we'll show you how to use them.

Your objective is to get the journalists to report on what you are doing in such a way as to reflect your desired message. So you need to understand how to catch their attention, to provide them with complete, useful information and to generate interest on their part to tell your story the way you want it told.

Journalists might create their own version of your story, using your materials as background, or they might simply use your material. I was trying to get a publication to include a review of one of my books, and they were playing hard to get, complaining how little time they had to write a review. They had read the book and liked it, but they just couldn't fit in the review. I said, 'Would it be helpful if I sent you some material?' 'Oh, yes!' So I wrote a glowing review, sent it to them and they published it verbatim! Obviously they agreed! No, I won't tell you who it was! But it just goes to show, sometimes you get lucky.

Way 36   Produce a press kit

A press kit is usually a folder or some other nifty container (I've seen 100-page loose-leaf binders and large cardboard boxes called press kits, for example). This contains a selection of goodies for the press to use in reporting on your story. If you use a folder, bear in mind it will probably end up in a filing cabinet, so make sure it's not awkwardly shaped. If it won't fit their storage systems, they may put it where it will fit – in the waste basket.

A typical press kit should contain:

- The latest press releases (make sure the old, out-of-date ones are pulled before you send one out to someone new).
- A backgrounder (see Way 38)
- A fact sheet
- Perhaps some reprints of stories that have already appeared
- Photos with captions
- Biographical notes on personalities involved
- A 'Q & A' (questions and answers) sheet
- A brochure
- Perhaps an annual report of the company involved
- A catalogue
- A sample of the product, if feasible
- Maybe a specification sheet
- Other devices designed to make the kit memorable and to encourage its use.

Revise the press kit whenever it seems appropriate. (Make sure you date everything, even photo captions.)

Your objective is to make sure that everyone who is in your key audience in the media has an up-to-date press kit. This can even be a reason to phone or visit the journalist.

If you are sending the press kit through the post, include a covering letter to introduce the triggering event that prompts you to supply the kit. Highlight a story angle. Send it to the journalist by name, not just 'Features Editor', and follow up after a few days with a phone call to make sure the kit was received. Then you can offer further information and help to sell your story.

Way 37 Issue a press release

A press release should be about news. It should have a sense of urgency to it. If the news is time sensitive, you may have an embargo date on it, eg: 'Not for release until after 2 pm Tuesday, 4 July'.

The release should be no more than two or three pages of double-spaced typing, with a compelling headline and introduction, accompanied perhaps by a photo. Make sure the photo has a caption, and that the press release has a contact point (names, phone and fax numbers). Your objective is to get some ink – a story, or at least a mention – in the publication. Maybe the release will prompt a call from the publication asking for more information, resulting in a story that goes into more detail.

People who receive press releases get maybe 20 or more a day. So don't expect yours to be read all the way through at once. First, you have to get their attention! The headline and the opening paragraph are the most important words on the page.

A good press release quickly answers the journalist's immediate questions:

- Who?
- What?
- When?
- Where?
- Why?
- How?

Think about what kind of story the publication is looking for. Does your release deliver? It must.

What would a press release for this book look like? See page 48 for one approach, aimed at the marketing communications media.

Some press releases are basically for the record. They convey information about a company's activity that is not particularly newsworthy in its own right, but that a business journal such as *The Financial Times* or *The Wall Street Journal Europe* will publish as part of their mission to cover business activities within their realm of influence. Here's an example:

**Jacques Phlange Joins Eurobiscuits to Head
Human-Resource Management**

Eurobiscuits, which markets the *Biscuits du Paradis* brands, announces the appointment of Jacques Phlange to the position of Vice President Human Resources, effective June 25, 1992, reporting directly to Helmut Schwinz, President.

Mr Phlange has 20 years of multinational human-resources experience and was most recently Director, Human Resources, for Eurobrek Foods Benelux.

His responsibilities include spearheading the implementation of up-to-date professional human-resource systems throughout the division and leading the development and upgrading of its overall people capability. On his appointment, Mr Phlange said: 'My mission is to stimulate an organisational climate where we recognise that to be the biscuit market leader throughout Europe, and to meet all our other objectives, can only be achieved through people. People are the true value of our company.'

Mr Phlange, a Frenchman, is based in Brussels.

In these examples, I've left out the essentials, such as a letterhead, contact names, dates and so on. They must be included, of course.

Way 38   Produce a backgrounder

A backgrounder will have a longer shelf-life than a press release. It's a story or article that goes into the subject in some depth. Its purpose is as its name suggests, to give background to the message.

A backgrounder on this book would go into the need for a manual on getting publicity and would distinguish it from other books on the market, for example mentioning its own strategy of practising what it preaches. It would go into examples of this in more detail. It would talk about the audience and their current economic environment. It might quote several people – for example one or two potential readers on why they have a need for publicity and the difficulty they have in knowing how to go about getting it.

Getting Publicity Made Easier – New book *101 Ways to Get Great Publicity* practises what it preaches
(Way 37, Issue a press release)

Ink. That's what it's called. Publicity. It's been said that any publicity is good publicity. And that there's no such thing as bad publicity.

But how do you achieve **great** publicity? Ink that works effectively for the task at hand? A new book, *101 Ways to Get Great Publicity*, by Timothy R V Foster, has been published that makes this its goal. **(Way 1, Understand your objectives)**. It's a book that practises what it preaches **(Way 7, Be relevant)**. 'I want this book to be the best-selling book on publicity ever,' said Foster **(Way 32, Go for the impossible dream)**. 'I decided to use as many of the 101 ways to get great publicity to get great publicity to make *101 Ways to Get Great Publicity* happen,' **(Way 3, Be strategic)** added Foster **(Way 41, Use a spokesperson)**.

This approach has already manifested itself in several ways **(Way 24, Run your programme or it will run you) (Way 21, Don't lie)**:

● A daily radio programme called *A Way a Day to Make It Pay* has been introduced, based on this and Foster's other *101 Ways* books **(Way 47, Use radio clips)** and linked to other programming **(Way 49, Hold a radio phone-in)**
● A research survey on the use of publicity by various organisations has been commissioned **(Way 9, Do some research) (Way 14, Support claims with facts)**

101 Ways to Get Great Publicity is aimed at people who run their own business or help others to run theirs, who are self-employed or involved with a charity or an organisation with a mission, or who just want to know more about getting noticed **(Way 2, Understand your audiences)**.

It is based on the author's 30 years of experience working for leading companies such as Procter & Gamble, Merrill Lynch and Burson-Marsteller, and as an independent consultant in the UK, Canada and the USA **(Way 10, Be an authority)**, and is published by Kogan Page (£7.99) **(Way 56, Write a book)**.

Press release checklist

Subject _____ Date _____

	Remarks	Who does it	Deadline
Copy			
☐ Research data	_____	_____	_____
☐ Brief writer	_____	_____	_____
☐ Edit, rewrite text	_____	_____	_____
☐ Translate?	_____	_____	_____
☐ Approvals	_____	_____	_____
Photos			
☐ Subjects	_____	_____	_____
☐ Sources	_____	_____	_____
☐ Select	_____	_____	_____
☐ © OK?	_____	_____	_____
☐ Copies made	_____	_____	_____
☐ Captions	_____	_____	_____
Production			
☐ Quantities	_____	_____	_____
☐ Design	_____	_____	_____
☐ Proofread	_____	_____	_____
☐ Copies made	_____	_____	_____
☐ Collating, binding	_____	_____	_____
☐ Delivery	_____	_____	_____
Distribution			
☐ Lists – who?	_____	_____	_____
☐ Mailing	_____	_____	_____
Follow up			
☐ Follow-up calls	_____	_____	_____
☐ Monitor media	_____	_____	_____
☐ Evaluate results	_____	_____	_____

A typical backgrounder might run for up to six pages of double-spaced type. As always, it must be dated and give contact names and numbers.

Way 39   Include a fact sheet

This is a brief (one or two pages) summary of key facts about the subject. If the subject is a private aeroplane, it would include dimensions, weights, performance figures, operating costs and the like:

Price:	£169,500
Engine:	Lycoming IO-540-T4B5
Prop:	McCauley C/S 3-blade
Seats:	4
Length:	24.9 ft/7.6 m
Height:	8.4 ft/2.6 m
Wing span:	32.8 ft/10 m
Maximum weight:	3,260 lbs/1,479 kg

etc. (Note that the dimensions are shown in both Imperial and metric – it's a good idea to stay flexible.)

If it was a computer, it would have lots of technical information, such as:

Microprocessor
- Motorola MC68000, 32-bit architecture
- 7.8336 MHz clock speed

Memory
- 1 or 2 Mb of RAM, expandable to 4Mb
- 512k of ROM
- 256 bytes of parameter memory

etc. (Note that jargon is okay here – it does not need to be explained.)

If it was a drug, it would have indications, eg:

Prevention of re-infarction
- Reduction of the danger of further thromboses of the

coronary vessels in persons who have survived cardiac infarctions.

With a fact sheet might go drawings or diagrams of the product, or flow charts showing how the subject fits in to its surroundings, and so on, eg:

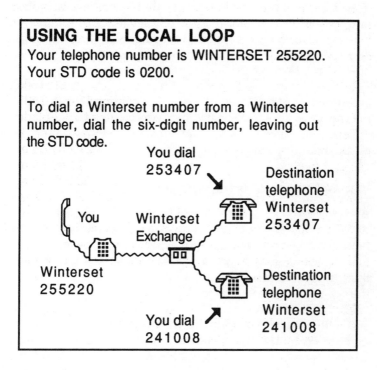

USING THE LOCAL LOOP
Your telephone number is WINTERSET 255220.
Your STD code is 0200.

To dial a Winterset number from a Winterset number, dial the six-digit number, leaving out the STD code.

You dial
253407
Destination
telephone
Winterset
253407

You
Winterset
Exchange

Winterset
255220

Destination
telephone
Winterset
241008

You dial
241008

Way 40   Use a Q & A sheet

A question and answer sheet is a good way to address a complex subject. It poses the questions most likely to be asked by the journalist and the ultimate reader and handles them in an easy-to-understand way, for example:

Q Can one become used to or dependent upon (brand)?
A No, there is no danger of becoming used to or dependent upon (brand). This has been clearly demonstrated in long-

term studies on re-infarction and thrombosis prophylaxis and in research on the long-term use of (brand) by rheumatism patients.

Well, easy to understand for the ultimate reader of the resultant article, who in this case is a doctor or pharmacist!

A Q & A can help explain a topic that is hard to grasp. It can also be helpful in stimulating a story on the part of the journalist, by identifying different angles or points of view. A good Q & A should provoke the reaction: 'Oh, that's interesting, I hadn't thought of that!'

It goes without saying, but I'll say it anyway, that the answers must be absolutely correct. This means they should be checked, double-checked and verified by the client and appropriate experts. It's a good idea to get a signature and date on the final draft to confirm this has been done.

Way 41　Use a spokesperson

A spokesperson is often an employee of the client company or its PR agency. However, in many cases, especially those with a large technical content, the spokesperson may be an outsider, usually someone with acknowledged expertise. Using a qualified and recognised outsider also provides the benefit of third-party endorsement (see Way 5).

The spokesperson must be trained to speak knowledgeably about the subject at hand in an informative and articulate manner (Way 42). He or she will participate in press conferences (Way 43), interviews, media tours (Way 48) and may write articles (or at least byline articles written by a professional writer).

In selecting a spokesperson, it's a good idea to resolve to have just one for any given area or subject. This person should be knowledgeable and credible in the eyes of the audiences. An insider will probably be a senior executive of the organisation. An outsider, regarding the subject matter, will probably be a professional, perhaps the author of a book or articles, or be a broadcaster, or in some other way be noted for his or her expertise. The candidate must also have strong communication and presentation skills.

Way 42   Use media training

Spokespeople should be trained to handle a variety of interviews. In such a programme, which typically lasts a half or a
full day, they'll go through a structured process designed to
develop their experience and comfort level under various
scenarios. The objective is to help the participants to understand the settings (eg, a TV studio, a 'stopped on the street'
intrusion, a friendly chat, a hostile interview, and so on),
become accustomed to cameras, flash bulbs, lights and micro-
phones thrust under the nose, know how to establish credibility, understand how to control the flow of questions and
answers, and learn to communicate the message effectively in
a range of interview situations.

A well-trained person might evade an awkward question
and refocus on the core message by saying: 'I'm glad you
asked me that. However, the question you *should* ask is
whether we...' and then go on to say what needs to be said.
An untrained person would respond with: 'Er, yes, er, no, er,
you know, er, what was the question again?'

Media training is offered by various organisations, some
that specialise, others that have it as one of their services. Most
major PR agencies offer it, and so do quite a few video
production companies.

A good media training programme doesn't just provide
rehearsals of interviews. It also includes research into specific
issues that are likely to surface, a review of existing media
relationships, a consciousness-raising session that educates
trainees about the media and their motives, and an intensive
message-development session. The idea is to build a track that
meets the spokesperson's needs and those of the specific
media.

The training session involves intensive role playing, videotaped to enable critiques and improvements to be measured. A
good trainer will bring in real-live journalists to play the
interviewers (quite likely the person who delivered the news
the night before on one of the TV networks).

Focus will be on familiarisation with the message, so that it
will always be communicated effectively, no matter what the
cue.

Way 43 Hold a press conference

When you have something important and newsworthy to communicate, and you want to reach a lot of people all at once, hold a press conference. These are events that run up to an hour in length and are staged to present some statement of significance. They usually end up with questions from the floor. The very nature of the press conference technique can promote a sense of immediacy and importance.

A typical press conference will have several presenters, led and moderated by a senior person, or possibly the PR adviser, and making use of the spokesperson, if different. Each person might speak in ten-minute chunks, addressing their particular issue.

Where is it held? It can be at a hotel meeting room, at the client's or its PR agency's location or at some other conference-oriented venue, such as a club. If the conference is linked to a major event, such as a trade show, there will be press meeting rooms laid on by the organisers.

You need to make sure there is enough room for the number of people expected, with public address system, slide projectors, videos – whatever tools are needed to tell the story. If there is to be a product demonstration or introduction, you should think about how this will be revealed at the moment of truth – instil a little mystery into the proceedings! There should be the facility to serve refreshments as required, depending on the time of day.

As to the time of day, you must bear your desired result in mind. Remember, journalists work to deadlines. If you want something on the noon news, don't hold the press conference at 11 am – you need to give them time to write it up. If you want the news to break in the evening papers, tell your tale in the morning. If you want it in the morning papers, tell it at midday or early afternoon, but remember that the electronic media can scoop the papers. Basically, the rule is to use the most appropriate time for the media you invite.

Send the invitations out a couple of weeks in advance, if possible. The invitation should state the purpose of the press conference, identify all the presenters, and give the obvious details like time, date and location. It's a good idea to follow up with a phone call nearer the event to make sure your invitees will attend and to sell the idea of coming to the doubters.

It's a good idea to notify the Press Association (85 Fleet Street, London EC4P 4BE, telephone 071-353 7440, fax 071-936 2363) about an important press conference. They publish a daily news diary of important events demanding coverage, which is seen by all the major national and regional newspapers and other media. See *The Media Guide* (Way 4) for other press agencies.

Be prepared to circulate materials to those who don't attend. These would include any handouts at the event, plus possibly transcripts or a tape of the presentations. Handouts at the event would be the latest press kit plus anything directly pertinent to the subject.

After the event, if there is time, it's worth while contacting the journalists who came to make sure they have what they need, and to answer any questions.

The content of the press conference should be scripted to ensure that each presenter knows what to say and when, and that the messages come across clearly. Rehearsal is absolutely essential, ideally on-site. It helps to put everyone at ease, and contributes to a smooth event. This is also the opportunity to make sure the gadgets (mikes, slides, etc) all work. To be really strategic, you should develop and practise possible questions and answers at the rehearsal.

On the page overleaf is a checklist you may find helpful.

Way 44   Hold a photocall

If you can come up with an appealing or offbeat picture, you can greatly increase your chances of getting good coverage. Shots of Prime Minister Margaret Thatcher picking up rubbish in a London park made it into the newspapers. Unfortunately, so did the story about how her aides carefully laid out the debris beforehand, so that it could be picked up using the best camera angles.

But seriously, folks, a lot of creative time is spent by PR people trying to come up with good photo ideas. Olympic Gold Medal swimmer and Cadbury's Chocolate Break spokes-

Press conference checklist

Subject   Date

	Remarks	Who does it	Deadline
Venue			
☐ Location picked	_____	_____	_____
☐ Reserved	_____	_____	_____
☐ Sound system	_____	_____	_____
☐ Projector (type)	_____	_____	_____
☐ Video (type)	_____	_____	_____
☐ Computer (type)	_____	_____	_____
☐ Autocue	_____	_____	_____
☐ Lighting	_____	_____	_____
☐ Room layout	_____	_____	_____
☐ Refreshments	_____	_____	_____
☐ Photographer	_____	_____	_____
☐ Site signs	_____	_____	_____
☐ Parking	_____	_____	_____
Event			
☐ Participants	_____	_____	_____
☐ Scripts	_____	_____	_____
☐ Slides, videos	_____	_____	_____
☐ Rehearsals	_____	_____	_____
☐ Handouts	_____	_____	_____
☐ Exhibits, displays	_____	_____	_____
☐ Staffing	_____	_____	_____
Invitations			
☐ Invitations	_____	_____	_____
☐ Lists – who?	_____	_____	_____
☐ Mailing	_____	_____	_____
☐ Follow-up calls	_____	_____	_____
Follow up			
☐ Post-event calls	_____	_____	_____
☐ Monitor media	_____	_____	_____
☐ Evaluate results	_____	_____	_____

man Duncan Goodhew swimming with the dolphins to launch Swimathon wasn't bad (see Way 7).

'Relevance with a twist' is a good way to describe an ideal photo opportunity. Children and animals always work. Page-three girls do sometimes. Someone in a wheelchair overcoming great odds is good. Look in the business section of the quality papers: there's the chairman of a brewery downing a pint, the CEO of British Airways with a huge model Concorde under his arm, the head of an auctioneers standing beside a picture that just sold for $40 million. You get the idea.

Way 45 Do video vox pops

A vox pop is a 'man/woman in the street' interview. It's used to get a collection of reactions from a random sampling of people to a particular question. You collect an array of these, and then edit them together to make a stream of response that tells your story.

Here's how you do it. You hire a camera crew (see Way 58) – usually just a camera operator and maybe a sound person – and set up your tripod in a suitable location. You may have to ask permission if you are using a particular shopfront as a background, but if you are just in the street with no particular background, don't worry about it. If you see a policeman nearby, tell him what you're doing. He'll probably help. If he turns nasty, pack up and go somewhere else. Some places, inside shops, malls or arcades, airports, mainline rail stations or museums, for example, definitely require permission. Some may even want a fee!

Then you stop people as they walk by and ask if they'd mind answering a question: 90 per cent of people intercepted will agree to this invasion of their privacy. You very quickly tell them what you want, where to look (at you, not into the camera). You stand just to one side of the camera, holding the microphone for the person you're talking to. Tell the person what you're going to say, then proceed. What you don't want are yes/no answers, so the way you phrase the prompt is very important.

What kinds of words do you need? Structure your prompt to get them to say what you want to hear.

Let me show you. I recently directed an informational video on the subject of BS 5750 – the BSI's (British Standards Institute) quality affirmation standard. We were doing vox pops in Oxford, with the objective of getting various people to give some peculiar answers as to what BS 5750 meant to them. We wanted to show that not many people even knew what BS 5750 was. We were not expecting too many people to say, 'Oh yes, that's the BSI quality standard' (nor did they). We wanted to hear odd things. We eventually managed to get, quite extemporaneously, examples like: 'A hormone for cows?' 'A new TV channel?' 'Some kind of new car?' However, I started asking people: 'Does the term BS 5750 mean anything to you?' and I got a whole bunch of very polite (this was *Oxford*, after all) 'I'm afraid not', 'No, nothing'. Then I changed the technique to saying, 'I'm going to say something to you. I want you to repeat the words and if they mean anything to you, tell me what they mean. If they don't, tell me what you think they *could* mean'. And that's how we got the answers we wanted. In fact, we did get one person who knew, so that's how we started the story.

Way 46 Use a video news release

A video news release (VNR) is the television equivalent of a press release. It is a short piece of video that is provided to television programme producers with the objective of their using it in their show. It gives them pictures and sound without them having to go to the trouble and expense of creating it themselves. A VNR is distributed either on tape, by landlines or via satellite. It's paid for by the client – the TV station gets it free. The station makes no payment, nor should it charge to run it.

A VNR is news oriented, and so is usually produced to resemble a newsclip on a typical news programme. Some VNRs go so far as to use a newsperson on camera who comes across exactly like a 'real' network newsperson – standing in front of the location holding a mike, saying words to camera, and signing off with a legitimate- sounding 'Bradford Lepage, Newcastle upon Tyne'.

Expertly produced VNRs will also feature 'B-roll'. (The 'A-roll' is the primary 'news' footage.) B-roll is extra footage (cutaways and establishing shots) that is supplied, usually with a written script, to enable a local station to integrate the extra scenes into their own programme more seamlessly.

The VNR is sent primarily to news programme producers. If it has a special-interest application, its distribution can be more tightly focused. For example, a release about a new weedkiller would be sent to shows dealing with gardening or home matters. One about a new style of contact lens might be aimed at a health or a fashion show. But both of these would also find a place on an early-morning or daytime magazine programme.

VNRs have been around for several years, and are becoming increasingly accepted by broadcasters, many of whom pooh-poohed the very idea that they might introduce some images not from their cameras in the early days.

There are companies that distribute VNRs via satellite. An example is Visnews (now Reuters Television), based in London. They have their own satellite, and most TV stations throughout Europe have a permanent link to this, since Visnews is a major provider of news footage to TV stations throughout the world. So it is a simple matter for them to send a message to the target producers advising them of the VNR that will be available on the 'bird' at four o'clock this afternoon. If the producer is interested, he or she instructs the station people to tape the programme when it is aired, so that it can be reviewed and possibly used.

There are no guarantees that such footage will be used, just as is the case with a press release. So the more interesting and compelling you can make it, the better chance you have of getting aired.

How do you know if it got used? The best solution is to videotape the target programme. This presents a bit of a challenge if you are aiming at 33 stations throughout Europe. There are broadcast monitoring agencies in some areas, however, that claim to record *everything* that is broadcast on all channels, all the time. You can contract with them to provide you with the footage you need (not an inexpensive process). An alternative would be to make sure than an ally (your local salesperson or dealer?) in each target location records the relevant programmes and reports back on results. You should also ask the station if the material was used and when (most will be decent enough to tell you), but it will be harder to get a piece of tape of the programme with the on-air proof back from the station.

Steve Garvey, Corporate Television Manager at Visnews, says, 'The key to success in placing a VNR is planning ahead to get the most targeted distribution possible. Placing stories with broadcast programme makers who are genuinely inter-ested in your subject will get you the best results.' If you know that a certain programme airs and would be interested in your material, you should tailor scenes to meet their needs.

Back in 1986, the BBC was one of those who raised an institutional eyebrow at the very thought of using something so American as a VNR. Then Reagan bombed Libya, and the American tourists stayed away from Britain in droves. Burson-Marsteller in London brought a VNR production crew over from New York and made a VNR in Britain, targeted at American newscasts, with the objective of showing the folks back home what a jolly place Blighty was for a holiday, even now. The VNR was sponsored by a British airline, a hotel chain and a car-rental firm. We had all these Americans in pubs and walking through touristy places (and walking into the spon-sor's hotels and coming through the airline's gates) having a merrye olde time. The result? Placement on every prime-time network newscast in the US, *and* a four-minute spot on Auntie BBC's main news showing what the British tourist industry was doing to bring the Yanks back over. It's all a question of relevance.

Way 47   Use radio clips

You can develop radio clips from your vox pops (Way 45). An audio release is similar to the VNR mentioned above, except it's just sound. As such, you must be mindful that the end product is radio, so simply taking the soundtrack off the video may not work.

An audio release is typically a 30-, 60-, or 90-second tape produced for distribution to radio stations. Essentially it's a press release on audiotape. It might include a narrator and a brief interview with your spokesperson, or it could be structured so that the spokesperson provides answers and the local radio station is provided with a script of the questions. Then the local announcer can give the impression that a live interview is taking place. This must be dealt with most carefully. The late, great Benny Hill did a wonderful skit in which the questions and answers got out of sync, with predictable results!

There are people who specialise in placing this sort of material with the stations. I did one of these when I produced my video, *Your Guide to Antique Shopping in Britain*, a few years ago. The end result, in fact, was that the tapes we sent prompted interest on the part of the stations, which then wanted to do their own phone or live interviews. The actual tapes were never used. But we got the desired result – exposure on radio. So radio clips can be a means to an end.

Way 48   Do a media tour

A media tour can be very effective. This is where the spokesperson tours the country (or the continent, or the world) and meets up with print and broadcast media people in key locations, giving a series of interviews. It must be carefully planned and coordinated to maximise effectiveness. Because it saturates the media with interviews it helps to obtain a concentration of communications in a very short time.

You'll notice the results of a media tour if a celebrity suddenly starts appearing on a variety of local media over a one- or two-day period. It's very prevalent with movie stars plugging their latest films, or authors their books. And it can be just as effective with a spokesperson discussing a new car burglar alarm or dietary food product.

Start planning a media tour well in advance by picking a good time-frame. If it's about a new book, will the book actually be in the shops when the author is in town? Will the product be available?

Then pick the locations strategically. In what sequence should they be visited? Are there any local events that will get in the way of good media coverage? (There may be a big football match or parade or something that could take over and prevent good coverage for your story.)

What are the most important media to hit? The local TV talk show, a popular radio programme, the local evening paper? Which are they?

Contact the media and tell them the spokesperson will be in town on the given date, and work out an interview schedule. It will help to send a media kit to journalists on the list, with background information on the topic, and a biography and photo of the spokesperson.

In your initial contacts, you have to sell in the story idea. If there is a local angle, (eg, spokesperson born there, or went to school there) point it out.

You can see that there is a great deal of skilled planning and execution in a successful media tour. It requires diligence and excellent follow-up skills.

Needless to say, the spokesperson needs a detailed itinerary of the entire schedule, with all the facts – dates, times, locations, names, addresses, subject angles, and notes about the interviewer. To send a spokesperson on their own to do a media tour is cruel and unusual punishment. Ideally an aide should go along to take care of details and the inevitable screw-ups.

If you want a record of the broadcast interview, take a blank cassette along and ask for the show to be recorded. If you don't do this, it's very hard to get one later.

Follow up by contacting every interviewer to confirm that the interview was broadcast (if not live) or covered in the press. Ask for tapes or articles not already obtained.

Media tours can be great. They are very hard work, and they are not cheap, what with travel and lodging expense as well. So don't go into one with your eyes closed.

To eliminate the need for extensive travel, however, there's a new twist, the *satellite* media tour, which is being offered by Corporate Television Networks of London. CTVN is in partnership with Independent Television News (ITN). In this arrangement, the spokesperson simply goes to ITN's studios (or some other location with television link-up facilities). A segment of satellite time is reserved, perhaps one or two hours. The network of 'media tour' stations is advised of the availability of the spokesperson and invited to reserve interview slots within the available time segment. Then two-way live interviews can be conducted. These may be transmitted by the receiving station live or taped for inclusion in later programming. A whole tour done in a couple of hours! Again not cheap (probably at least £3,000–£5,000), but think of the time saved.

Way 49   Hold a radio phone-in

This is where your spokesperson appears on a radio talk show as an expert. The host fields questions from listeners and the spokesperson answers them. It's a good technique when they have established expertise, and it can be a good way of ensuring they get on the air.

To arrange this, identify the programme you want your person to be on, then contact the programme director of the station concerned. It's like placing a story, really. You'll need to supply things like press kits and perhaps an audiotape of the spokesperson in action, or some other supporting material, such as a copy of their book.

As with the media tour, if you want a copy of the show, you'll need to arrange your own recording of the result by supplying a blank tape to the station and asking them to record the programme.

Way 50   Have a telephone hotline

It probably doesn't cost British Telecom a great deal of money to have its own freephone 0800 numbers. So they've come up with a good thing. It's called the Business Information line (0800 444 111 – see Way 4). Here, you get a recording which is really a mini-documentary radio programme. The one that's on as I write is a 7½ minute talk about relationship marketing. It quotes a couple of professors from the Cranfield School of Management and shows how the effective use of telecommunications can help a business to improve and maintain good relationships with its customers. It ends up with an invitation to call another free number to get more information. I wonder how many other companies can afford to offer unlimited 8-minute freephone calls to deliver their message to the public?

Nevertheless, even if you are not BT, a telephone hot line is a good approach to supporting your story. Increasingly you will see consumer products inviting feedback from customers by having them call their 'information line'. This should, of course, be a freephone number (0800 on BT, 0500 on Mercury). Just having the dialogue is a form of publicity, because it serves to reinforce the image of care and open communications.

If you want to make money while delivering your message, you could use a premium-rate telephone service. These are the 0891, 0898-type numbers where the caller runs up a bill at the rate of over 50p per minute at peak time. The newspapers are full of ads for such services. There's a whole industry serving this type of operation, and they even have a premium-rate telephone number you can call to get information about how to get on the bandwagon. In fact, they also have a premium-rate *fax* number to call so you can get a printout of the scheme!

Way 51   Use advertorials

An advertorial is paid editorial. It's a section in a magazine or newspaper that is clearly labelled 'special editorial' or maybe even 'advertisement', but that resembles the layout of the publication, more or less. The message is delivered in a series of articles, often supported by real ads. *The Wall Street Journal Europe* does this sort of thing whenever there's a big telecom fair in Budapest or somewhere. *Time* magazine does it all the time. So do *The Times* and *The Financial Times*.

That's why you'll see huge chunks of the broadsheet newspapers devoted to 'Industry in Kuwait' or 'Aerospace'. The extent of editorial that is actually paid for varies with the publication and subject matter.

Advertorial sections are welcomed by most publications because they get an opportunity to attract advertisers they may not traditionally get. The whole section can, of course, be reprinted, and then it becomes further grist for the handout mill, press kits and that sort of thing.

An advertorial is usually arranged through the advertising sales people of the medium. They often have people whose entire role in life is to develop these sections, so it's a well-travelled road.

Creating Your Own Media

A great deal of publicity can be generated from communication tools you create yourself. With the advent of desk-top publishing (DTP), anyone with a reasonably sophisticated computer and a laser printer can produce respectable-looking materials for circulation to their audiences.

DTP means you can design the materials right on the computer screen, if necessary using trial and error until you end up with the look you want. If you don't have this equipment, there are plenty of DTP bureaux that do. In fact there's a whole cottage industry out there ready to serve you. Look in the *Yellow Pages* or the *Thomson Directory* under 'Typesetters' or 'Desk Top Publishing Equipment and Services'.

If the budget allows, of course, there are full-service agencies that will create, design and produce your printed materials. Look under 'Designers – Graphic'.

Way 52   Offer a brochure

A brochure is an alternative to reality. It is the equivalent of the free taste you get in a good cheese shop. It provides continuity from the moment of contact to the moment of taking on the proposition. So it represents the product or service until it has been acquired or employed. It must reassure the target that this will be good. It must describe the *benefits* in glowing terms, creating desire. It must impart some of the same feelings as the real thing in an appetising way. It must ring of the same quality as the end product. It must inform and be a reference point (including the provision of things like technical specifications, dimensions, addresses, phone and fax numbers, and so on).

When your target wants to take action, the brochure must

make it easy to get to a successful conclusion (business!). Ideally, it should then become a hand-me-down, finding its way as an unsolicited testimonial into the arms of one of your targets' friends, perhaps with a recommendation to use the subject matter.

My advice on brochure copy is that it should be written with your target audience's interests in mind, not your client's. Not, 'We offer the finest tyres', but, 'If you seek the finest tyres, you'll find them here...'. Use a compelling statement as a key opening headline: 'One call gets all your ribbons, diskettes, paper and supplies delivered FREE overnight and saves you up to 71%!' from a mail-order catalogue for Viking Direct). Much more motivational than: 'Your number-one office supplies house'.

If the brochure is intended to be informative and educational, give it an appropriate title, eg, 'The Royal Mail Guide to Successful Direct Mail' or 'Make Communications Make a Difference' (from BT).

Way 53   Produce a newsletter

If you develop a mailing list of clients, prospects and the media, a newsletter is a good way of keeping in touch and showing that something is going on. Here's where DTP comes into its own, because it can keep your production costs way down. If you have your own DTP equipment, but you are not skilled at design, my advice is to have your newsletter professionally designed and formatted as a first step. Then your own DTP set-up can be used to create a good-looking piece by obeying the initial design concepts evolved for you.

The newsletter keeps people informed of new developments, refinements in product lines, new customers, nifty ways of using the product, special offers and so on. If you want people to save it for reference, punch holes in it so it will fit in a binder (if it's A4, use four holes so it will fit in either a four-ring or a two-ring binder). You may want to distribute a binder with the first issue, or offer one on request, to keep costs down. Somebody ordering a binder will be a very good prospect!

You might want to invite the recipients of your newsletter to reproduce articles free, provided they give acknowledgement to the source. To keep tabs on this, I advise you to ask them to contact you for permission to use any text or illustrations. Then you can build a file of placements that have resulted, so you know how effective the newsletter is at communicating.

A good newsletter will help you or your client to build a relationship while offering extra opportunities to get publicity.

Way 54   Produce a magazine

If the budget will stand it, the next step up from a newsletter is a purpose-built magazine. What's the difference? I'd say a newsletter has just a few pages, say, typically, 4, 8, maybe up to 16. A magazine is more likely to have at least 24 pages. It may even carry ads. Another way of looking at it is the cover. Does the publication have heavier cover stock than the text pages? If yes, I would call it a magazine. I'm looking at an example of a magazine right now, from BT. It's called *Business Issues*, and it comes out quarterly. It has heavy cover stock, lots of colour and white space, yet only 12 editorial pages. Here's the table of contents:

- Up front – Editorial (1 page)
- Anatomy of a customer – Your complete guide to understanding customers and keeping them loyal (2 pages)
- Service secrets – Discover the true importance of customer service (2 pages)
- Feeding off feedback – How customer feedback can boost your sales (2 pages)
- All in a day – The working day of a customer information manager (2 pages)
- Questions answered – Advice on your most important customer care queries (2 pages)
- How do you score? – Your customer service rating (1 page)

It also has a folder in the back cover for a special-purpose brochure, in this case, one called 'Business Solutions – Using communications to gain more business from your existing customers'.

A lot of organisations produce 'house magazines'. These may be aimed at employees or beyond. The typical house magazine has all that soft stuff like, 'Maisie in accounts is getting married' and 'Helen in process control had a baby boy'. These are of little interest outside the organisation. But other house magazines may have a specific communication objective, such as helping to move the corporate quality programme forward, or sharing sales ideas.

I produce a quarterly for Burson-Marsteller called *Euronotes*, which is aimed at internal audiences. Its stated objective is: 'To provide our people with a useful, actionable interchange of ideas and experiences. It is intended to help you serve your clients better by bringing to your attention activities in other offices and throughout Europe, and to help you get to know our resources and people better.' When we did a powerful write-up of the Brussels office, their manager, Jan Robberechts, ordered extra copies and circulated them to his customers and prospects. This resulted in actual new business.

Way 55   Write an article

Professional writers are always looking for opportunities to write and be paid for it. I came across a journal called *Telecom World*, another BT publication. This is sold on a subscription basis, aimed at the technical side of telecommunications. I contacted the editor, Justin Quillinan, and suggested that, since I specialised in technical subjects, I might be able to write some material for them. He asked me to send him some samples of my work, which I did. The result? 'We'd like to do a story on *you!*' he said. So another writer, Steve Homer, was commissioned to interview me and the story appeared in the December 1991 issue. It was called 'Fax and Figures'. The sub-head went on: 'For business people who work from home, the fax has become as indispensable as the telephone, enabling users to send documents instantaneously to locations across the world. Tim Foster, a businessman whose domestic fax is rarely quiet, evangelises about the power of the fax, and why he believes good communication is the key to success in business.'

The article ran to one and a half pages, and was supported

by a full page colour photograph of yours truly peering mysteriously over the cover of my newest book, *101 Ways to Generate Great Ideas*, which was picked up again on the run-on a couple of pages later. Talk about getting great publicity!

Placing an article in an appropriate magazine is not particularly difficult. You may want to have it bylined by your spokesperson, or by the managing director of your client, or by the brand manager of the product. This provides them with a platform where they are seen to carry some clout on the subject. The secret of success in this area is to know your medium and know your journalists (see Ways 4 and 11). If you have a good idea of what the publication covers, designing a story to appeal to their readers should not be hard.

When you have the concept, if you don't know who to phone, send the editor a fax saying something like: 'Would you be interested in an article about..., written by..., one of the foremost authorities on the subject? Please let me know to whom I should address this within your organisation.' Then follow up with a phone call a day later: 'It's about the fax I sent yesterday...' This should result in a name. Then you contact the name and say: '(Editor) suggested I contact you about etc.' This should at least result in an invitation to submit the article. Get the names of the personal assistants and secretaries as you speak to them and become their allies. Include them in the action: why the story is interesting, why the writer is special, how important it would be to have the story in the publication and so on. They will help you to drive the story on to the pages of the publication.

When I made the video *Your Guide to Antique Shopping in Britain*, I was interviewed by the editor of *World of Antiques*. This ended up as a two-page article in the magazine about why I did it, and the philosophy behind the programme. Then the story became part of the sales presentation, to show the retailers the coverage we were getting. Later I placed an article in *Retirement Living* which was basically a modification of the video's script. We offered the tape in a sidebar and sold dozens.

Way 56   Write a book

I do a talk at seminars called 'Write a book about what you do'. I suggest it is absolutely the best way to become an acknowledged leader in your area whom people seek out for advice! To start, answer these questions:

- What is my objective?
- What is the book about?
- Who will buy it?
- What needs does it fill?
- What does the author bring to the party?
- What should it be called?
- Who should publish it? (Go and look in bookshops and see who publishes similar books.)

Then prepare to sell it, armed with the answers to the above seven questions. Write the table of contents. Write single-paragraph descriptions of each chapter, and write at least one chapter.

Forget agents. They are mostly *useless* for this kind of work. I've never had an agent able to sell a book on my behalf. Most of them don't even want to look at what you do, because they're 'too busy'. Yet I've sold 14 different books on my own, working directly with publishers.

So write to your target publisher. I started my relationship with Kogan Page with a fax to Philip Kogan (whom I did not then know) which resulted in him requesting a copy of the manuscript within 20 minutes of getting the fax. He got it within an hour (biked), and bought the book two days later (that was *101 Ways to Succeed as an Independent Consultant*).

If you don't know whom to contact, telephone and ask for the name of the person to write to, and send a one-page descriptive letter, with this information:

- The proposed title
- The target audience
- The rationale/need for the book

- The chapter headings
- How many words you expect it to be
- The style – paperback, coffee-table, etc
- How many illustrations
- When and how you can deliver it (floppy disk, ms paper, etc)
- Your price ideas
- Your timetable
- The author's credentials – CV, copies of articles, etc.

You may not make a lot of money writing a book, but the mileage you can get out of it is worth all the aggro.

Way 57 Distribute flyers or handbills

One of the earliest forms of getting publicity is to hand out flyers on the street, stick them through people's letterboxes, put them under car windscreen wipers and so on. A friend of mine, Sue Collinson, started a successful second-hand children's clothes business this way. She DTP'd a flyer and handed it out to mothers when they were picking their children up after school. They flyer told about the shop and invited people to come in and sell their old, quality clothes. By handing it out to the right audience at the right time, she turned what is essentially a shotgun technique into a finely targeted rifle shot.

Way 58 Make a film or video

Professionally produced videos usually end up costing in the region of £1000–£2000 per minute of running time. So a ten-minute video could cost between £10,000 and £20,000. It can be done for less, but the lower cost will show up on the screen. Quality is not cheap.

That said, videos can be very effective communication tools, because they use the most powerful medium, television, to tell their story. And they can be a disaster if done badly. Who hasn't suffered through an excruciatingly produced corporate video? The problem is, your audience, when looking at television, are comparing your video with what they saw on the box last night.

Forget your hand-held home-video camera. You need proper equipment, lights, tape format. Most productions these days are shot on Betacam, although some are still done on BVU (broadcast video U-matic). S-VHS is also becoming popular.

You start the process with a briefing session in which the communications objective, audiences and messages are all made clear. What is the tape for? How will it be distributed? Is it to be shown on a 16-screen video wall at the World Travel Market at Olympia, or is it to be sent out to people wanting more information? Will it be shown by the sales people to prospects when on a sales call? Will it run, unattended, in the lobby of the client's building? What are the deadlines?

This kind of briefing is given to a production company, and you may invite competitive bids. You should ask for a treatment, which is a few pages outlining the creative approach the company proposes, and a budget quote. They will need an idea of what sort of budget you are working with. You can find these companies listed in directories such as *Broadcast Production Guide*, or through the International Visual Communications Association.

Such companies will have a *showreel*, with examples of their work. This will help a lot in making your decision. What is most important is track record and trust. Do you feel the people you meet are the kind you want to handle your job? A good indication is the amount of repeat business the company has had with good clients. They don't get repeat business when they screw up.

Michael Rodd, former presenter of BBC-TV's *Tomorrow's World*, is now chairman of Blackrod, a video production company he started in 1980, which has become one of the top five in the UK. His advice to would-be programme producers is: 'When you offer a production for bids, ask to meet the actual team who will work on your production. Some companies represent themselves just through sales staff, and when it comes to the actual job you find yourself dealing with strangers. You have to feel comfortable about working in *partnership* with the creative people, because they don't know as much about your business as you do. Do they have the ability to understand the basics of your business? Do they have the simple journalistic skills to grasp your points and communicate them effectively? Look for enthusiasm and the desire to be involved in the entire process. If a company just wants to go ahead and do the job without you, watch out!'

Some productions can be made using existing footage, perhaps artfully combined with new material. If you have made a video news release (Way 46), or vox pops (Way 45), these could very easily find their way into your production if that would work.

A few years ago, I made a video for British Midland Airways to celebrate their fiftieth anniversary. We did not shoot one foot of film or tape. Everything was 'swipe footage'. In fact, for the early material, we had no motion pictures at all, so we had to use the skill of Ken Morse and his rostrum camera to create movement out of still pictures. And I used old newsreel footage from the Visnews archives showing the introduction of the Spitfire (which happened the year BMA's predecessor company was founded) and other 1938 flying scenes, like Wrong Way Corrigan, to set the stage. There's always a solution on video!

Involving Others in Your Message

Remember what we said about the value of third-party endorsement (Way 5)? This section is all about identifying and enlisting the aid of third parties to get you great publicity.

There are all kinds of people out there who would help your cause if given the opportunity and the right sort of motivation. They might share your interests, or agree with your message, or be satisfied users who would be happy to evangelise on your behalf. In some cases, you won't have to pay for this – not directly, at any rate (although you may need to cover their expenses, such as travel and food, etc). There are celebrities who will help if you make a donation to their favourite charity or provide some other quid pro quo, like giving them an opportunity to plug their latest book, film or record.

And let us not forget those who are more directly involved – the people we call stakeholders. They can often be enlisted to enthuse about your story, quite naturally, if they have been treated right over the years. So let's start with them.

Way 59   Understand stakeholders

Stakeholders are people who have a stake in the outcome or success of whatever you are involved in. They include people like these:

- Employees
- Families of employees
- Retirees
- Families of retirees
- Members of the local community

- Local government officials
- Suppliers
- Employees of suppliers
- Families of employees of suppliers
- Vendors and dealers, the trade
- Employees of vendors and dealers
- Families of employees of vendors and dealers
- Customers
- Employees of customers
- Families of employees of customers
- Shareholders
- Advisers to shareholders, financial analysts

Anything you are doing in the way of getting publicity should acknowledge the impact of the activity on stakeholders. Perhaps variations on your theme can be tailored to the stakeholders' needs. Perhaps they should get advance notice of activities. You don't want key people finding out about things from the newspaper, radio or TV, when you could have told them yourself, do you? If you want them to feel special, you have to treat them as special.

Way 60   Appeal to special interests

Does your message affect any special-interest groups? These are people who can be grouped together and identified as having a concern about a specific issue. Sometimes they are called pressure groups.

They may already be organised, such as Friends of the Earth, National Anti-Vivisection Society, Vegetarian Society, Help the Aged, or Campaign Against Racist Laws. (There is a book called the *Directory of British Associations*, available at your public library, which provides the latest lists.)

Or they may not yet be organised, presenting an opportunity. Suppose your message is of interest to a group of people, but they are not organised together in any way. What would it take to organise them? Simply finding one or two people who would *really* be affected by your message would be a good way to start. Talk to them about their concerns. Ask them if they feel there is a need to convey this message to the public. Suggest the formation of an entity to represent this point of view, etc.

Assuming, then, that a special-interest organisation exists, how do you enlist their aid in getting publicity for your cause? By showing them that your cause is *their* cause. Making that connection can involve ingenuity and perhaps an apparent leap of faith. For example, some organisations want to outlaw the advertising of cigarettes, or smoking in public places. Others, even some non-smokers, want to protect the freedom of choice in our society. They don't want more and more restrictive laws. See how these two points of view can be represented?

Way 61   Involve a celebrity

Involving a celebrity is a very common way of getting publicity. That's because it works. The London *Evening Standard* ran a story about how classy restaurants in New York give away left-over food to the homeless through an organisation called City Harvest. The headline? 'Homeless share leftovers from De Niro's table'. The story had photos of Robert De Niro, Liza Minnelli and Sylvestor Stallone, on the grounds that they ate at the restaurants that donated food to City Harvest.

Getting a celebrity to cut the ribbon and open your new supermarket is one of the oldest tricks in the book, but it will give the event a little more excitement than just opening the doors.

How do you get a celebrity? You work through their agent. One of the most prolific of these is Noel Gay Artists, in London, representing such people as Rowan Atkinson, Harry Enfield, David Frost, Stephen Fry, Hugh Laurie, Esther Rantzen, Tony Slattery and Emma Thompson. To find agents, look in the *Yellow Pages* as follows:

● Actors see Theatrical and Variety Agents
● Authors see Literary Agents
● Models see Model Agencies

- Musicians see Concert Agents
- Performers see Entertainment Agencies

Way 62   Involve a charity

It seems the words 'link to charity' are engraved in every publicity proposal I've ever seen. By having a charitable beneficiary, the likelihood of getting good media coverage is enhanced, because who would be so cold-hearted as not to be seen to support a worthy cause?

To find charities, the good old *Yellow Pages* come through again with the heading 'Charitable Organisations'. There are also the *Charities Digest* and *Voluntary Agencies Directory*, both available at your public library.

The charitable link could be that a donation is being made to the charity for every item sold, that the proceeds are going to the charity, that people are encouraged to do sponsored runs, walks or other tests of endurance for charity.

Another advantage of this approach is that the charity may in itself have communication networks and mechanisms to help promote the event or activity, thus, once again, supplying third-party endorsement.

Way 63   Involve a politician

Politicians need friends, too. They often have agendas that could be seen to align with your own. When the film I directed on the BS 5750 quality standard was launched to the public, there was a preview screening at London's Café Royal. David Frost moderated (he was in the film) and Baroness Jean Denton, who was the Minister for Small Business in the Department of Trade and Industry, made a speech.

The way to involve a politician is to find one whose message is aligned with yours, bring this to their attention, and take it from there. Write to them at the Houses of Parliament, or wherever they hang their hat.

Way 64   Involve royalty

In spite of the generally bad press they have been getting for the last few years, royalty is still good for publicity. Their most common involvement is the royal patronage of an organisation, for example, the Princess Royal and the Save the Children Fund, or the Princess of Wales and the AIDS charities. There are also special-interest projects, such as the Prince's Youth Business Trust (Prince of Wales). Any organisation with the word 'royal' in its name undoubtedly has a royal patron. And many others do, too.

To find out which royal goes with which charity, get a copy of *Royal Patrons* from the Charities Aid Foundation, 48 Pembury Road, Tonbridge, Kent TN9 2JD, telephone 0732 771333. It's £5.95, including postage, and updated regularly. It lists the charities according to each royal, then it cross-indexes the charities alphabetically.

Remember, the royals don't need publicity, but they are generally happy to support a cause that they are already involved in. In most cases, royal involvement is arranged through the executive of the relevant charity. Anything over six months' notice of the need may be risky, since the royal schedules can change quite quickly.

A good entry point, if you are starting from scratch, is to contact the Lord Chamberlain of the Queen's Household, at Buckingham Palace, London SW1A 1AA (071–930 4832) and outline what you have in mind.

Nigel Douglas, the opera singer, organises musical soirées for people needing very upmarket entertaining. He recently ran a concert at Winchester School which was in support of the Winchester Cathedral Trust, whose patron is the Duchess of Kent. She attended, dropping in by Queen's Flight helicopter, so the audience, whose host had paid for them to attend the concert (proceeds to the Cathedral Trust), had the pleasure of her company and a little shoulder rubbing.

Way 65   Involve a sportsperson

Sportspeople are generally so disgustingly healthy they can do a lot in the realm of conferring perceived health benefits on a product (swimmer Duncan Goodhew and Cadbury's Chocolate Break, for example, see Way 7). As with performers, they usually have agents, and the granddaddy of such agencies is

IMG, The International Marketing Group, with offices all over the world.

Once again, selecting the sportsperson has a lot to do with the kind of sports your target audience is interested in. The candidate should ideally be a role model for your audience.

What will be the involvement? Will it be as spokesperson (see Way 41)? As user of the product and thus endorser (see Way 5)? As adviser to the company (see Way 67)?

Way 66 Involve an animal

Animals can be great to help convey your message, but you obviously have to be careful. Merrill Lynch in New York's slogo was: 'Merrill Lynch is Bullish on America'. (Bullishness in the financial world denotes positive expectations.) Our TV commercials featured bulls and even our corporate logo included a stylised bull. The St Louis office moved to new premises and somehow, some nut managed to bring a full-sized, real-live bull into the brand new office (a huge, open-plan area that covered thousands of square feet). This was thought to be an excellent photo opportunity – a great big bull standing among all the desks and computers in the new high tech office, with its acres of freshly loomed, seamless carpet. Need I say more? The entire carpet had to be replaced after the bull decided it was not *just* a photo opportunity.

Candy Newman, head of Animals Galore, trains animals for use in films, commercials and such. She did that TV commercial for the Solid Fuel Advisory Board – the one with the big dog, the cat and the mouse, all lying comfortably in front of a nice warm fire. She says: 'If you're going to use an animal, keep what you want to do within the realms of its natural activity – it's just more feasible. And introduce them to their human co-stars well in advance. A human can fake liking an animal, but if the animal doesn't like the human, they won't lie. There's always that element of unpredictability with animals; they can ad lib quite well. One time, we had some bright red macaws as background for the launch presentation of a new brand of colour film – the bird was part of their logo. They were perfect in rehearsal, but when the client started his speech, extolling the virtues of the new type of film the birds would not shut up. They screeched and generally strutted around, stealing the show. The louder he spoke, the louder they screeched. It certainly made it memorable.'

Way 67   Create an advisory board

An advisory board of experts in your field can be very helpful. They might help in designing the message, the product, the communication, the sponsorship, all kinds of things. If they are seen to be important in the area of interest, they can confer gravitas to the project that might otherwise be hard to get.

An advisory board is particularly useful in the early days of a product's life cycle. The lifelong experience and know-how of the advisory board replaces the inexperience and lack of track record of the actual subject. The members of the board can be good interview subjects, each taking a different angle of the overall story. But do remember to train them (see Way 42).

Way 68   Use allies

Maybe you can make up an alliance of like-minded people. That's what the beverage carton industry did in Europe. Through Burson-Marsteller they established the Alliance for Beverage Cartons and the Environment. It is composed of paperboard manufacturers and cardboard carton makers. It exists to tell the story of carton packaging in an atmosphere where some environmentalists are hostile to the idea of landfill being used to dispose of empty milk cartons and the like. They think reusable glass bottles are more environmentally acceptable.

The Alliance story is interesting, because it explores further points of view. For example, the energy lost in transporting heavy empty bottles around, and washing them with boiling water is greater than the energy that can be gained by burning the cartons in an energy-generating incinerator. Cartons can also be recycled into such things as egg cartons. On such things is legislation based.

So who are your allies? How can they be brought together to tell a cohesive story?

Way 69   Involve customers

How can you involve your customers in getting great publicity for you? It needs to be a win/win situation. If you've been doing great work, your customers should be happy, and probably won't object to helping tell your story.

If you make a video, you can vox-pop your customers (see Way 45) and then edit them together to make your message sing. You can use their fan mail in your promotional material. How about putting up a big picture frame of satisfied-customer letters in your reception area? If you have a journalist doing a story about what you do, you can invite them to interview a customer or two. You can invite them to speak at a seminar you're putting on. Your satisfied customer can sell your services better than you can.

Way 70   Involve suppliers

Enlisting the aid of your suppliers in telling your story presents interesting angles. For example, some companies have very high standards for the organisations that supply them – Marks & Spencer leap to mind. Now that many companies are becoming registered under the BS 5750 quality standard, they are often demanding that their suppliers be similarly registered.

Is there a story about how your supplier worked in partnership with you in developing a solution that you now offer? This sort of item works very well in the trade press.

A good way of involving your suppliers is to give awards. Ford Motor Company, for example, have their Q1 Award, which they give to suppliers that meet extremely rigorous quality standards. The winner of the award hangs the plaque in their reception with pride. So the annual selection of award winners becomes a good trade-press item.

Way 71   Involve employees

You quite often see framed pictures of the 'Employee of the Month' in corporate offices. Domino Printing Sciences, the company that makes the ink-jet printers that mark the sell-by dates on various consumables, such as cans of Coke, have a massive employee recognition programme, involving nominations, presentations, pictures in reception and engravings on the plaque. The annual winner gets an all-expenses-paid trip to one of the company's subsidiaries, such as in the US, to exchange points of view with their opposite numbers across the sea.

The people get their names and pictures in the local newspaper as well as the house magazine. It's all part of the process that identifies a company as a caring organisation, a good place to work, and thus obviously a good place to patronise with your business. See how, layer by layer, you build up the story?

Way 72   Involve the community

How can you involve your local community? Well, it depends what your message is. When it was announced that British Coal was to close dozens of mines and throw 36,000 miners out of work, the local communities staged a protest jaunt to 10 Downing Street. There's a lot of power in this kind of grassroots mobilisation. The closures were deferred, largely because of the massive protest march and the ensuing uproar of indignation.

There are more positive involvements, too. How about getting the community involved when you're going after the next Olympic Games, or you want a new underground railway built, or you want a new traffic-light system? Let me count the ways.

Way 73   Involve the family

The family is one of the stakeholders (see Way 59). How can you involve them? Whose family? Yours? Your client's? Your client's customer's?

Suppose you were designing an event to which you wanted to attract men in their late thirties and forties. You can only hold the event on a Saturday. How can you be sure to get the men out? By involving the family, you'll make it easier. So make sure there are rides and other activities for the kids.

Then it becomes a 'Dad's special outing'. Mum will be delighted.

Air shows are supposed to be where you go to watch aeroplanes being flung about the sky by daredevil pilots, or to look at rows of rare birds parked for easy photography. Then why do they have bouncy castles and merry-go-rounds? So it becomes an event for the family. There is no excuse for not coming.

And of course, a small part is being played in the educational/motivational role of turning the kids on to aviation for the future.

You can have contests for kids that are designed to have them bring their parents along when they go to see if they've won a prize, and there, surprise, surprise, is a message for the grown-ups. Life insurance anyone? Timesharing? You have been warned!

Way 74   Get signatures

One ploy that never seems to go away is the old 'get signatures' routine. You take a position at a well-travelled location, set up a card table and some signs and stop passers by. The objective is to get thousands of signatures to plead for some change – yes this, or no that. Get enough signatures and not only do you have something to deliver to city hall, Number Ten, or wherever, but you've probably got a nice photo opportunity and at least an item in the paper.

Way 75   Create a coalition of like-minded people

When you are collecting signatures, you have a splendid opportunity to enrol supporters of your cause in a coalition or special-interest group so that you can more powerfully bring pressure to bear on the offending parties.

When I lived in Bucks County, Pennsylvania, a bunch of us got together over a new sewage treatment plant that was going to be put in a green belt area next to the Delaware River. We played the role of NIMBY (not in my back yard). We had all kinds of stories running in the local press about that, thanks to the different points of view we were able to present, and killed off the plan.

Way 76   Use ambassadors

There are a lot of very valuable people out there just itching to be of further service. The retired in particular can be excellent ambassadors for your cause, especially if they have expertise in the area of interest.

A few years ago, I made a video news release (see Way 46) for Jaguar Cars, USA. They were celebrating the fiftieth anniversary of the Battle of Britain at the world's biggest air show at Oshkosh, Wisconsin. They had a purpose-built tent, with a Messerschmitt 109, a Hurricane and a Spitfire on display (as well as some classic E Jags). The display was put on by the RAF Museum at Hendon.

We needed a spokesperson to get interviews on TV, radio and in the press and hired Battle of Britain veteran Pilot Officer William Walker, a Spitfire pilot who had been shot down in 1940. We brought him over to the USA for two weeks to visit the Smithsonian Air & Space Museum as well as Oshkosh, acting as Jaguar's ambassador. He was wonderful, appearing time after time on talk shows and other interviews. He had also been chairman of Ind-Coope Breweries for some years and was happy to point out that his company car had been a Jaguar.

Way 77   Involve an expert or specialist

There's nothing like a bit of expertise to set the theme. So if you are launching your new cooking oil, why not demonstrate it in the hands of the world's foremost fish and chip cook? Who is that? I have no idea, but it's the sort of outlandish title you can create. A new camera or film might employ the services of a famous photographer to show how it's done and to lend a bit of credibility.

How do you pick up an expert? People who are recognised by their peers within their fields qualify. It might be the author of a book (see Way 56), or the winner of an award (see Way 83), or the top-earning golfer, a motor-racing champion or an

Olympic Gold medallist. It might be an inventor, or the recently retired head of a corporation with vast experience in the field.

People wanting to demonstrate burglar-proof security devices have hired former burglars. Let your imagination roam! When we made the film about BS 5750 quality registration, we interviewed executives of companies that had recently gone through the registration process, as well as officials of the British Standards Institute. If you are writing an article or a book, there's nothing like a quote from an expert to establish its authority.

'Using an expert enables you to increase both the perceived and actual value of what you do,' says Martin Langford, chief executive of Burson-Marsteller's London office and chairman of the Public Relations Consultants Association. 'That's why we make a point of bringing the top people in their fields together to address the needs of our clients. It's a practice that goes a long way in strengthening the results of our work.'

Designing Special Events

By staging an event, you can generate a high level of publicity – and a lot more. The event might be a symposium or seminar, a screening, a party, an activities day or something else. It is, by definition, different from the run-of-the-mill activities we encounter day-to-day. It is special. Let's look at some of the options.

Way 78   Hold a symposium or seminar

This is a technique often used by pharmaceutical companies that want to reach doctors. Many doctors, particularly specialists, have to take a certain amount of instruction each year to maintain their qualifications so, by holding a learned symposium, an organisation wanting to discuss the latest science of heart disease or migraine, for example, can attract plenty of specialists. The drug company can sponsor the entire symposium, or can take on a side-role of holding ancillary meetings, perhaps off-site, during the run of the main event, which in itself might be running under the aegis of the relevant professional association.

Trade shows are a good place to hold seminars. Some of these have a seminar programme built in. There may be a charge for this or not. You could arrange to make a presentation on your special area at one of these, or you could hold your own event, either in your own exhibition stand or at one of the venue's meeting rooms.

Richard Birtchnell, managing director of London's Forum Communications, has organised hundreds of seminars and conferences. He says: 'If you are going to charge for attendance, you must be seen to be objective. People will resist paying money to attend what they perceive is a sales presentation. It's a very good idea to link up with the relevant trade publication for the discipline. They will give the event credibility, they can write it up and promote it in their pages. Their participation will also help to attract speakers, and will ensure after-the-event coverage. The way to get maximum advantage from a seminar is to make sure that the keynote speaker or chairperson is one of your people. This heightens your visibility.'

You can invite the press to the seminar. If it's a technical subject, invite the relevant trade press. This should be good for some coverage in their magazine.

Way 79   Hold a screening

A private screening of a new film can make you good friends. When I worked in New York nobody did this sort of thing better than *Time* magazine. They would invite their advertising clients to private screenings of the latest films, just before they came out. These would be supported by the finest canapés and refreshments, and very low-key smooth talk (no 'pitches') from the personal advertising rep who looked after my account. I saw *Jaws* three days before it hit the street. And *Marathon Man*. It's nice to be treated as if you're important. You don't forget.

Way 80   Throw a party

Got something to celebrate? How about a party? There are plenty of interesting locations. In our jaded society, you often need an off-beat venue to attract your audience. If the place can be relevant to the client, so much the better. Visnews, the TV news-gathering organisation, held their Christmas party at the Museum of the Moving Image. You can hire places like the RAF Museum at Hendon or the Museum of Natural History in London, or various stately homes, such as Goodwood House or Brocket Hall, or castles such as Leeds Castle.

Link it to charity (see Way 62) and there could be extra mileage in it for you (and the charity).

Way 81　Hold a teleconference

This technique is very effective when you have to convey the same message to large groups of people in different locations. You gather the groups together in an array of venues and link them all together via live satellite television.

There are several ways of structuring this. In order of ascending cost, they are:

- One-way TV from a central originator to several locations
- As above, but with two-way sound between each location, so that people at outlying spots can communicate live with the originator
- As above, but with two-way video between each location, so that people at outlying spots can communicate live and be seen as they do so.

Teleconferences are extremely effective for needs such as reporting an organisation's financial results, giving the opportunity for investment analysts in New York and Tokyo to question the chairman in London. They're also a handy way to launch a new product, especially one that has high-tech overtones.

Video Arts, the training film company, held a teleconference at the Grosvenor House Hotel in London a couple of years back. John Cleese (one of their founders), gave an address on the use of humour in training. This was followed by an interactive Q & A session from places as far apart as Manchester and Malta. They charged a fee for attending (which included a dinner), and while guests were waiting, showed excerpts from their latest films. The place was full. Which shows that you *can* get away with charging people to see a sales pitch if you have someone with the powerful appeal of John Cleese available.

Stephen Watson is managing director of Corporate Television Networks Limited, a London-based company that organises teleconferences. He says: 'Before you decide to use a teleconference, it's intelligent to conduct a cost/benefit analysis to compare this approach with other communication systems. Such options include making and distributing videocassettes or perhaps installing a permanent, satellite-fed internal TV network. The choice of teleconference site is important, too, because some locations have the satellite and video equipment already permanently installed, making it less expensive, easier and quicker to arrange.'

Way 82   Hold a contest

A contest can enhance the appeal of a promotion. With the right sort of prizes, you can get good publicity, especially if you link the prizes to the media. For example, when I did a radio appearance on Radio Sussex to promote my video *Your Guide to Antique Shopping in Britain*, we gave away some free copies of the tape. Radio Sussex is in Brighton, a Regency town, so we invited people to phone in to the station and name a year that fell in that era. Winners got a tape. Giving the tapes away helped us to get the air time.

Look in the press. You'll see some kind of contest going on every day, usually headlined with the offer: 'Ten free videos to be given away!' So if you want to promote something, work out what you have got that can make a nice prize. Then make a deal with the medium for the prize to be awarded in return for some paltry gesture (which, incidentally, gives your cause the publicity you seek), *et voilà!*

A lot of competitions these days invite you to ring a premium-rate telephone number (eg, 0898) with the answer to a 'skill'-testing question, like: 'Is red a colour of the rainbow, yes or no?' You call the number (at a cost of perhaps 50p or more) and give your answer. Then they draw names from a hat to see who won. No doubt the premium-rate phone not only covers the costs, but is profitable.

Way 83   Give an award

Everyone likes to win an award. It might be simply 'best mum in the street' or 'best essay'. If it's a form of professional recognition, so much the better. Go into the reception area of any good video production company and you will find plaques, statuettes, cups, goblets and platters galore, acknowledging the fact, for example, that *The Generating Game* won the

1989 IVCA (International Visual Communications Association) Award of Excellence in the Corporate Image Category, sponsored by *Audio Visual* magazine (produced by Michael Kann Associates for the Central Electricity Generating Board).

PR Week, the journal of the public relations industry, holds the annual *PR Week* awards programme. This offers recognition in 23 categories, plus the Grand Prix. The categories are:

- Outstanding individual contribution
- Consultancy of the year
- Best in-house department
- Best regional consultancy
- Best new consultancy
- Best investor relations campaign
- Best international campaign
- Best business campaign
- Best consumer campaign
- Best healthcare campaign
- Best corporate community involvement campaign
- Best non-commercial campaign
- Best promotional campaign
- Best use of research
- Best political campaign
- Best employee communications
- Best use of design
- Best use of photography
- Best use of video
- Best use of sponsorship
- Best annual report
- Best crisis management campaign
- Best staff development programme

Many of these awards are sponsored in turn. The outstanding individual contribution award, for example, (won in 1992 by

Des Wilson for his handling of the Liberal Democrat election campaign) was sponsored by the Mistral Group, a consortium of consultancies. A team of judges looks at submissions (each of which had to be accompanied by an entry fee). They make their choices, and then the whole event is staged at a suitable black-tie dinner held at the Grosvenor House Hotel. It's entirely self-supporting. (There's no such thing as a free dinner.)

Says *PR Week* editor, Stephen Farish: 'Holding an awards programme of this type helps position *PR Week* as the key journal of our industry. It provides an opportunity for us all to highlight good practice and to give recognition where deserved. We aim, with these awards, to set a benchmark for quality. Our judges are very demanding, and will bypass a slickly produced submission for one that demonstrates strategic thinking, wisely spent budgets and concrete results.' Another thing the awards programme enables is the production of a fat issue of the magazine, well supported by advertising, to report on the awards event! The issue becomes a useful reference work for the future.

If the event has enough 'legs', it can become a media extravaganza as well. In 1992 BAFTA (British Academy of Film and Television Arts) held its first awards programme for television (and cinema) commercials. This was staged at the Albert Hall and was sponsored by *The Sunday Times* and British Sky Broadcasting. David Frost was the host and, just like the Oscars award ceremony, there were all these people in black ties or gowns receiving their statuettes. Excerpts from nominated commercials were shown and the winning commercial in each category was screened in its entirety. The whole programme was videotaped and presented the next day on prime-time television on the Sky One (satellite) channel.

Almost every industry has (or could have) an awards programme. Here are a few others:

- The Best Factories Awards (*Management Today*)
- The British Housebuilder of the Year Awards (New Homes Marketing Board)

- Drinks Advertising Awards (*Off Licence News*)
- The Financial Services Advertising Awards (*Money Marketing*)
- The IPA Media Award (Institute of Practitioners in Advertising/*Campaign*)
- The MacUser Awards (*MacUser*)
- The National Media Mind Competition (*Media Week*)
- The Recruitment Industry Awards (IPA/Institute of Personnel Management)
- The Travel Awards (*Travel Trade Gazette*)

And let us not forget the Nobel Peace Prize, endowed by Alfred Bernhard Nobel, the man who invented dynamite (get it?). Actually, the Nobel Foundation awards four other prizes as well, for physics, chemistry, medicine and literature. Is there an award for your industry? Want to start one?

Way 84   Buy up the house

If you really want to make a noise with your audience, how about buying *all* the tickets to an event and holding a special function? Then you will have their undivided attention, and they'll talk it up. This philosophy includes acts like hiring Concorde for a supersonic trip so you can make a presentation over the public address system on the way back from Mach 2.

Way 85   Have a booth where the crowds are

As you wend your way wearily through the rush-hour crowds at a mainline station, you will occasionally find display booths with incredibly enthusiastic people handing out free samples or inviting you to step inside and try one, or otherwise experience the new and interesting.

If commuters are the people you want to reach, this can be an effective technique. How would you develop a photo opportunity to get some media coverage of this? Think about it. If you've read this far, you should be able to come up with some ideas (see Ways 59–77).

Way 86 Participate in a trade show or exhibition

Just about every special interest has some kind of trade show or exhibition, and there are plenty of shows that cross borders and cover a variety of interests.

If you want to be part of the 'state of the art', these are the places to be. A well-organised trade show will have its own press office, giving you the opportunity to offer media materials. If you want to hold a press conference, they'll set it up for you. You can bet the media covering your area will be there, so it might be appropriate to arrange interviews or a scheduled visit to your booth.

At a lot of shows, the exhibitors will have a private entertainment suite at a nearby hotel where high-level entertaining can take place. You have special invitations and hand them out to the people you want to attend. The challenge is to keep the suite action lively. If your people have to stay there 14 hours a day for five days in a row, they can get pretty stale. So think of ways to keep things fresh.

Way 87 Have a 'total experience/activity' day

You may have seen these advertised (by the organisations that offer the facilities). These are events where a company can bring its key audiences, customers, star salespeople, or the media, for example, to a location where they can experience such delights as driving a formula 1 racing car, going up in a hot air balloon, gliding, parasailing, skydiving, and so on.

After you've given the people an unforgettable experience, you marshal them into the marquee and show them your slides or whatever your pitch is. No, actually, you do it the other way around. Sell to them first, then entertain them. Otherwise they'll try to sneak out before you run the commercial.

To use the process effectively, identify the kind of event that would appeal to your intended audience. You'll see ads in *PR Week* and *Marketing*. A fashion show where they get to do the modelling? A visit to a flight simulator, to try out a new Airbus? There are lots of things the Walter Mittys inside us want to do. *You* can make it happen and make friends for your message, too.

Suitably relevant invitations wouldn't be bad, such as a mock airline ticket for a hot-air balloon ride. But be careful! A friend of mind sent out what were essentially sealed baked-bean-type tins containing invitations to a shop opening. The tin had a teaser on the outside and invited the recipient to open it for a nice surprise (the invitation). The problem was, this was during one of those terrorist blitzes we've become so used to, and people were getting blown up by bombs in the mail. Nobody wanted to open their tins for fear that the surprise was less than nice! They called the police instead. What a palaver!

Using Stunts to Get Ink

It's just a publicity stunt! How many times have you heard that line? Stunts used to be the *basis* of publicity in the old days. You've heard of dance marathons? Flagpole sitting? Tightrope walking across Niagara Falls? The man who opened 100 oysters in 2 minutes and 22.17 seconds? Great publicity stunts, all. Thank goodness for *The Guinness Book of Records*, which lists so much.

People are still doing them. Parachuting off Tower Bridge or from the Whispering Gallery in St Paul's Cathedral. Bungee jumping. Climbing up the outside of the 102-storey World Trade Center in New York.

Way 88   Design a stunt

A good way to start designing a stunt is to think about something that might make *The Guinness Book of Records*. If you're not familiar with the book, browse through a copy and get a feel for the kinds of craziness people get up to. It is published annually, 'We do not publish gratuitously danger-ous categories, such as the lowest height for a handcuffed free-fall parachutist or the thinnest burning rope suspending a man in a strait-jacket from a helicopter,' it says in the introduction. 'Our main concern is to publish those records which improve upon previous records or which are newly significant in having become the subject of widespread and preferably international interest.'

The editor goes on to say: 'If an activity is one controlled by a recognised world or national body, that body should be consulted and involved in ratifying it.' They offer guidance by post about the breaking of records, if you send an sae at least a month before the attempt. Their address is Guinness Publishing Ltd, 33 London Road, Enfield, Middlesex EN2 6DJ.

If you're designing a stunt to get publicity, *please* try to make it relevant (see Ways 7 and 8)! And make it *visual*. If you want good coverage, there had better be a good picture there somewhere.

Avoid doing publicity stunts on days when there's going to be heavy news coverage of other events, such as elections, football cup finals or outbreaks of war. Stunts get good coverage when not much else is happening, but they aren't much good at edging out real news.

Way 89   Build a house

Suppose you arranged with a bunch of volunteers to build a house from scratch, and then have it donated to a charity for the homeless? Get the building supplies donated by local suppliers? Put up a huge sign showing all the entities that have donated cash or kind? You could have the ensuing activity covered by the local TV station and have a grand competition and opening ceremony, involving an appropriate personality (see Ways 59–77).

Way 90   Hold a sit-in

It's been said that if you remember the 60s, you weren't there. Well, I remember the 60s, and I *was* there. One thing I remember about the 60s was all those sit-ins.

Usually, it was a bunch of university students who went and occupied the library, holding up protest signs about the war in Vietnam or the like. Lately in the UK, it seems to be prisoners on gaol roofs, complaining about conditions and treatment.

With a righteous cause, a sit-in can be quite effective at generating publicity – like the commuters who refused to get off a train recently because they were tired of British Rail's treatment of them. They finally got some attention, plus a write up in the papers. How do you counteract this sort of thing if you're British Rail?

Way 91   Get arrested

My strategy for publicising this book is to use as many of the

101 ways to get great publicity to get great publicity (see Way 3.) But this is one way I *don't* intend to follow!

Nevertheless, a person of principle can use the law to make a statement. People not paying their poll tax leap to mind. But I have another theory: when someone says, 'It's not the money, it's the principle of the thing!' – it's the money! Most of the time.

Way 92   Go on a hunger strike

Here's another stunt I won't be using. But there are many examples through history of people refusing food to make a statement – even to death. It takes all kinds. Not recommended.

Dealing with Adverse Publicity

So far, we have been talking about generating 'great' publicity in this book. But what do you do when you want to combat not-great, that is, *adverse*, publicity? How do you make it go away?

The tabloids in the UK are notorious for savagely going after a perceived weakness and, like a terrier, not letting go until the unfortunate target drops to its knees. Ask the Royal Family. Ask many of the cabinet ministers of the last decade. Ask any fraudulent businessman. The weakness nearly always has to do with sex or money, or both.

Another aspect of the need to deal with adverse publicity is the propensity people have for sharing bad news more than they do good news. In my book *101 Ways to Get More Business*, I suggest that people share bad experiences four times as much as they do good experiences. I'm sure that equation applies equally to spreading rumours and tittle-tattle.

Way 93   Know what causes adverse publicity

Any kind of scandal, or hint of scandal, can lead you in the direction of adverse reports. These could include such matters as the chairman accepting a huge salary increase while the workers are being told they must tighten their belts, the managing director being caught kerb crawling in a red-light district, the financial director embezzling funds, the sales director offering bribes to a politician, a woman employee being fired because she wouldn't sleep with her boss.

Beyond scandal, there's just plain bad news. The company has to close a plant and lay off 3000 employees. Is this the sort of event that you want to leak out and be spread all over the papers before the employees are informed? Of course not. Yet it happens all the time.

Or the financial department made a mistake, and the production budget suffered a £60 million overrun before anyone found out – what could this do to the price of the shares?

Then there's some terrible accident, such as an explosion in the chemical vats, or a spill of toxic waste into the river.

Or maybe there's an extortion threat. Some criminal decides to poison your stocks of baby food in the shops, and will only tell you where the damaged product is in return for £1 million. And if you don't come through right away, he'll go to the media with the story, thus preventing it from being contained and dealt with.

Pressure groups can start rumours that become very costly to reverse. 'I hear that they've been having problems with their bottle sterilising system,' could do untold harm to a dairy.

And of course, the worst kind of publicity comes from being caught trying to cover up allegedly bad deeds in the hope that no one will notice. Most of the time the sin of the cover-up is considered to be much worse than the matter being concealed. Look at Watergate, Irangate, Iraqgate. Just the act of attaching the word 'gate' to the end of something serves to create an instant feeling that things are not as they should be. (Maybe that's what happened to the film *Heaven's Gate*, which actually made it into *The Guinness Book of Records* as the film with the largest financial loss!)

Bear in mind the smoking gun syndrome. There is always a memo lying around, or an ex-employee with information of a past problem which had been long forgotten or thought to be buried. The moment something awkward or important happens might just be the moment that person has been waiting for. Look at the problems US President Bill Clinton had in the early days of his campaign, with Gennifer Flowers alleging they had been having an affair for years. So the media say: 'And what else, Bill?'

Way 94   Know the cost of doing nothing

If you are faced with adverse publicity, you *could* ignore it and hope it will go away. I've got news for you. It won't. In fact it will get worse.

Consider these typical responses, and what they must do to the audience's perception of reported bad news. Jason Platypus, the managing director:

- Did not return phone calls seeking to verify this information
- Replied, 'no comment'
- Denied all knowledge
- Denied the event ever happened
- Said, 'I can't answer without my solicitor present'
- Said, 'I don't have time to talk to you now'
- Said, 'We'll probably issue a statement soon'.

Jason is digging his own grave, and the company's, behaving like that. The point is, the media report the denials or lack of availability factually, but the readers say, 'There's no smoke without fire, therefore: *guilty*!'

Way 95   Realise that negative publicity festers

Have you noticed how, when they think they're on to something, the media start looking in all directions to find additional fuel for the fire? Suddenly, the accused is found to be guilty of all sorts of related crimes, like living in a £500,000 mansion in the stockbroker belt, paid for and furnished by the company, being driven to work in a £100,000 chauffeur-driven Rolls–Royce, having taken Concorde to New York and back last week (£5000+ round trip), belonging to an exclusive golf club (£10,000 a year), having a daughter who lives in New York (in a $300,000 apartment on Park Avenue), having been expelled from school, having failed his O levels, having been fined £40 for speeding in 1976, having had dinner with his secretary – you name the innuendo, they'll find it, and if they can't, they may make some far-fetched claims. Notice how they always try to stitch a price to the item? This is designed to make people seethe with jealousy.

Then the media might start camping out on the subject's doorstep, shouting questions at every opportunity, forcing themselves on the victim, itching for a reaction, such as a punch in the mouth, that can go further to demonstrate how right it is they should pursue their quarry.

No matter whether the subject is guilty or innocent, what do you suppose is the damage that has been done by their delaying tactics? Keep reading the papers and you'll know.

Have you noticed how very nice the Prime Minister is as he or she gets out of his or her car at 10 Downing Street, in front of the press brigade, as it is relayed on the nightly TV news? There's always a smile and wave. It might be the only defence. But he or she certainly can't be accused of indifference to the media.

Way 96   Avoid adverse publicity

A lot of things that can cause adverse publicity can be avoided by a little forethought and strategic planning. Bad news from a company about its order book, its cost-overruns, its factory closures can all be dealt with proactively. A spokesperson can be named (Way 41) to handle the issues – don't forget the importance of media training (Way 42), a press conference (Way 43) can be called, a statement issued.

All this is best handled when the company has taken the trouble to . . .

Way 97   Be prepared

A lot of organisations develop whole crisis preparedness programmes designed to address the way they will handle communications if something terrible happens.

Many large public relations firms devote a great deal of energy and resources to serving this niche of the communications spectrum. Such programmes are developed by experienced counsellors and usually involve an audit or risk assessment, in which possible vulnerabilities are identified and discussed.

For example, an airline always has the threat of a fatal air crash hanging over it, so a complete written procedure on the communications process is established 'just in case'. Who does what, how the authorities and media are notified, what to do about passenger lists, how next of kin are to be informed and so on.

A continuous-flow glass furnace always has the threat of fire or explosion; a chemical factory has potential toxicity problems; a food processing plant has the threat of hygiene problems; a coal mine could have trouble down the pit. No industry or occupation is invulnerable. Even a firm of lawyers could have their safe burgled and their files rifled. So, be aware of what could happen and be prepared!

The development of a crisis-preparedness programme involves the identification and training of a crisis team. Roles are defined (who is the key spokesperson, who undertakes to notify the authorities, who deals with employees and so on).

Who should be on the team? Here are some ideas:

- Senior management person (decision maker)
- Operations/maintenance person (someone who knows how to turn things on and off!)
- A public relations person (in-house or out)
- Security person (who's used to dealing with 'the authorities')
- Personnel/human resources person (employee aspects)
- Medical resources
- Experts (if required)
  - Technical, scientific experts
  - Quality control person
- Diarist/secretary (to record what's going on)
- Photographer (pictures may be needed or useful)

One of the above should be designated as the official lead spokesperson, with others identified as back-up or support people (eg, experts).

The team's home addresses, telephone numbers, car phones, home fax numbers, pager numbers, all the stuff of keeping in touch in the 90s, should be listed.

The programme then generally ends up in the form of a reference manual. This should contain items such as these:

- Background on the company (written in lay terms)
  - Ownership (is it a subsidiary, privately held, a plc?)

- Locations of head and branch offices/factories, laboratories, etc
- Names of key officers
- Numbers of employees
- Descriptions of its lines of business
- Brief overview of financial results

The company background should also be tailored to each different location (eg, how many employees locally, what they make at this factory, the local corporate officers' names and titles, etc). This background material should be available in a form that will allow it to be handed out to the media if necessary, so of course it should be kept up-to-date (and *simple!*).

- The names of the members of the crisis team (with all their contact and responsibility details)
- The people/agencies (internal and external) to be notified in the event of a crisis (in accordance with the type of problem, eg a bomb threat has a different procedure from a fatal accident in the factory or a toxic chemical spill)
- The media contact list (names and media, phone numbers, etc):
  - Press agencies
  - Television newsrooms
  - Radio station newsdesks
  - Newspapers (national/local)
  - Trade press
- Draft statement in skeleton form to cover the main risk areas. (It is better to plan what you are likely to want to say when things are calm than to attempt to gain agreement on wording when a crisis hits.)
- An events log
  - Description of event
  - Date, time and place
  - Casualties (names, titles)
  - Results of event
  - Cause (if known, not speculative)
  - Employees involved
  - Who has been notified.

Way 98   Simulate a crisis

Once you have established your procedures, nominated your team, and generally steeled yourself for the worst, why not have a simulation session? This lets you test your teams and validate your procedures. It can be run for you by the organisation that handles your media training. I was involved in a crisis-simulation session that ran for a whole day, with a team of eight people undergoing all kinds of trials. It started off with the phone ringing and one of the people being told there was an explosion at their factory, with two or three possible fatalities.

The person taking the call gathered together the crisis team and they convened in a room we had specially wired up. There were phones, a TV, a radio and an interview room. Behind the scenes there was a control room, with trained media people who would phone up and ask for statements, interviews and so on at the most awkward times. An activist crashed into the room shouting obscenities about the company's operating practices. We had a weeping mother, wondering if her daughter was one of the people killed. The local mayor made complaints and issued threats. There were journalists who wouldn't take no for an answer and cameramen on the doorstep demanding an interview *now*. Every so often, we stopped the clock and discussed how things were going and what the team should do next.

The whole process took about four hours, ending up with a press conference. After this, the crisis team was given a break, while we feverishly prepared a simulated report to be broadcast on the evening TV news. One of our simulation team was a real TV anchorman, and we videotaped his news item. Then we invited the crisis team back in and played them 'the evening news', to show how well/badly they had handled the situation. Better to find out the realities here than in real life!

Needless to say, having been through the simulation exercise, the crisis team felt much better prepared to handle a problem should it arise – just as airline pilots do with their flight simulators, where they can practise all kinds of emergencies until they know what to do almost instinctively. Pilots keep practising. The crisis team should also keep practising, updating the issues and risks involved and updating its plans.

Way 99   Know the key steps in handling a crisis

Handling a crisis is straightforward if you have prepared for it. It basically involves following the manual.

There are two types of crisis. The one you know is going to happen (you're going to close a plant and lay off 3000 people), and the surprise (the explosion in Vat 9, that kills three people and the ensuing fire that spreads toxic fumes over the neighbourhood).

Dealing with a crisis that you know will occur soon should be easier than dealing with a surprise. Just follow the procedures you have developed. If you haven't developed any, get professional counselling or help!

Let's look at some typical steps in handling a surprise crisis. The biggest mistake is thinking that 'it's not that serious'. People should be trained to understand that if they have a problem they should report it to a member of the crisis team for action. Hoping something will go away, or that the universe will unfold in your favour tomorrow, won't work.

Something bad happens

- Problem may have surfaced directly to an employee's attention, or it may have been brought to their attention by an outside agency
- Collect as much information as possible
- If outside agency is pressing for action, take number and get back to them through crisis team
- Notify crisis team leader of the problem (as well as any other relevant agencies that should know at once, eg, fire brigade, ambulance, etc).

Crisis team takes control

- Crisis team gathers
- Assesses situation

- Prepares initial statement of what happened for both internal and external audiences
- Notifies the appropriate agencies (per procedure manual) that a detailed statement will be given (when and where)
- Meanwhile gives initial statement as required to both internal and external audiences. (This is important with 'notifiable' agencies, such as the police or health authorities, etc.)
- Determines strategy for short and medium term
- Prepares detailed statement and develops briefing sessions (eg, for media, employees, investment analysts, whoever)
- Conducts briefing sessions
- Manages the crisis, according to plan.

Way 100   Know what they want to know

If you have a good idea of what the media want to know, you'll be a long way to addressing your crisis. They want to know:

- What happened (detailed accounts of the event)
- Who's to blame
- The other usual stuff:
  - Where
  - When
  - Who
  - How
  - Why
- Who they can interview
- How they can get their cameras on site.

The key thing to bear in mind is that the media *will* get a story, no matter what you do. So who do you want in control of that? If you don't help, they'll start interviewing the man on the street, ex-employees with an axe to grind (see Way 93), unhappy customers, and so on. It's better to be proactive and in control than reactive as events escalate away from you.

Way 101 Handling the news beyond the team

All employees must be briefed and instructed on the communication protocols. Ideally, they should be asked not to discuss matters beyond a certain level of information, and that level should be provided for them. The switchboard and security people must be very high on the list of the well-briefed. They should have a statement available that they can refer to and read to a pushy journalist who is on hold.

Be very security conscious. You don't want prying eyes to see things they shouldn't. It's the innocuous things that can blow your story on to the front page, like extra photocopies lying around, faxing your plans to a competitor by mistake (yes, this has happened!), holding unguarded conversations in the lift, untrained secretaries (eg, temps) trying to be helpful and answering questions in the lunch hour when no one else is around.

If you treat a crisis in a businesslike way, you can minimise the effect of one when you have one. Remember Murphy's Laws:

- If anything can go wrong, it will, and at the worst possible time
- The situation will get worse.

'Ordeal by publicity is the legitimate grandchild of ordeal by fire, water and battle,' said George H Boldt in a 1954 address to the American Bar Association. The moral? Take control of your publicity or it will take control of you!

Index

activities day 87, 94
adverse publicity 99–108
advertisement 9
advertising 9, 10, 12, 35, 64
advertising agencies 9
advertorial 64
adviser 54
advisory board 81
agenda, hidden 24
agent 71, 77, 78, 79
Alambritis, Steve 21
Alliance for Beverage Cartons and the Environment 81
Allied Passengers Association 26
allies 12, 59, 70, 81
ambassadors 85
American Bar Association 108
angle 28, 38, 45, 81
animals 35, 57, 62, 80
Animals Galore 80
annual report 45
Apple Computer 36, 43
A-roll 58
arrest 97
article 10, 52, 69, 70, 86
arts, the 36, 39
associations, trade 12, 21
audience 9, 11, 13, 17, 23, 25, 26, 35, 39, 47, 80, 94, 101
audio release 60
Audio Visual 91
audiotape 14, 60, 63
audit 102
author 52, 77
authority 21, 47
autocue 56
award 82, 85, 90, 92

backgrounder 45, 48, 103
bad news 101
BAFTA 92
basics of publicity 9–34
BBC 14, 60, 73
Beaver, Paul 21
benefit 25, 66
Birtchnell, Richard 87
Blackrod 73
book, write a 1, 47, 71
booklets 37
Bookseller, The 29
booth 93
Boy Scouts 40, 42
brainstorming 17, 25
brand equity 35
brand manager 70
Brands Hatch 15
Branson, Richard 17, 41
briefing session 107
British Academy of Fim and Television Arts 92
British Airways 42, 57
British Coal 83
British Midland Airways 74
British Rail 97
British Sky Broadcasting 92
British Standards Institute 58, 86
British Telecom 15, 63, 67, 68, 69
broadcast 9, 12, 14
Broadcast 29, 30
broadcast monitoring 59
Broadcast Production Guide 73
broadcaster 52
brochure 14, 45, 66
B-roll 58
BS 5750 58, 78, 82, 86

bungee jumping 27, 96
Burson-Marsteller 33, 47, 60, 69, 81, 86
Business in the Community 42
Business Information Line 15, 63
Business Issues 68
byline 52, 70

Cadbury's Chocolate Break 19, 55, 79
camera crew 57, 105
Campaign 93
Capitol Hill 21
catalogue 45
celebrities 75, 77
chamber of commerce 12
Charities Aid Foundation 79
Charities Digest 78
charity 12, 43, 47, 75, 78, 88, 97
checklist, press conference 56
checklist, press release 49
cinema 9, 92
Civil Aviation Authority 23
claim 26, 32, 47
Cleese, John 89
clients 12
Clinton, President William 100
coalition 84
Cole, George 43
collecting schemes 37
Collinson, Sue 72
commercial 80, 92, 94
communication skills 52
community 41, 42, 75, 83
computer 22, 36
Concorde 43, 57, 93, 101
Confederation of British Industry 13, 19
conference 54
Conran, Sir Terence 40
consultancies, PR 10, 12, 42, 54, 102
contest 90
context 31
control 34, 53, 108
Corporate Angel Network 42
corporate citizen 41, 42
Corporate Television Networks 62, 89

cost/benefit analysis 89
Cranfield School of Management 63
credibility 32, 52, 53, 85, 88
crime reporter 21
crisis preparedness 31, 102
crisis simulation 105
crisis team 103, 104, 105, 106
customers 16, 35, 39, 76, 82, 94

Daily Mail 41
deadline 23, 49, 54, 56, 73
Department of Trade and Industry 13, 78
desk research 26
desk top publishing 66, 67, 72, 79
dialogue booth 15
dinner dance 43
Directory of British Associations 76
display 56, 93
Domino Printing Sciences 82
donation 10
Douglas, Nigel 79
Downing Street 83, 84, 102

Economist, The 29
editor 3, 70
education 36, 37, 84
electronic media 14, 54
embargo 46
employees 75, 82, 99, 103, 108
endorsement, third-party 16, 32, 52, 75, 78
endorser 80
entertainment agency 78
environmentalism 36, 81
errors 32
Euronotes 69
European Community 20
Evening Standard 77
event 14, 15, 26, 84, 87, 92, 93, 94
events log 104
exhibit 39, 56
exhibition 14, 94
expertise 21, 52, 63, 85

face time 10, 43
fact sheet 45, 50

facts 26, 32, 47
family 75, 83
Farish, Stephen 92
fax 15, 46, 64, 66, 69, 70, 71, 103, 108
Faxback 15
feature 25
Federation of Small Business 13, 21
film 72, 75
financial analysts 76, 89
Financial Times, The 20, 29, 46, 64
First Voice for Business 29
Flight International 21
floppy disk 15, 72
flow chart 51
flyer 72
focus group 26
Forum Communications 87
freebies 14
Freedom of Information Act 22
freedom of the press 22
freelances 12
freephone 15, 64
Frost, Sir David 77, 78, 92

gag order 22
games 37
Garvey, Steve 60
Generating Game, The 90
GMS Consultancy 20
goodwill 35
government officials 76
grass-roots mobilisation 83
Grosvenor House Hotel 89, 91
Guardian, The 16
Guinness Book of Records, The 96, 100

handbill 9, 72
handout 14, 55, 64, 104
Harvey-Jones, Sir John 16, 17
headline 19, 20, 27, 46, 77
health care 37
hoardings 10
hobbies 13
Home Run 29
horizontal publications 28
hot-line 14, 63
house magazine 69, 83
How to Get Sponsorship 39

How to Market Yourself as an Independent Consultant 22
hunger strike 10, 98

image, improving 35–43
improvement 27
independent consultant 12, 47
Independent Televison News 62
in-flight magazines 15
influencer 12, 13, 35
initiative 31
Institute of Personnel Management 93
Institute of Practitioners in Advertising 93
interests 13, 77
interim management 20
International Air Tattoo 32
International Marketing Group 80
International Visual Communications Association 73, 91
interview 22, 33, 52, 53, 61, 62, 70, 81, 82, 94, 105, 107
invitation 56, 95
involvement 75–86
IPA Media Award 93
irrelevance 19
issues 35, 106
IVCA 73, 91

Jane's Defence Weekly 21
jargon 50
journalist 16, 21, 22, 23, 32, 44, 45, 51, 52, 53, 55, 62, 74, 82, 108
journalists contact log 24
journals 14

keynote speaker 88

landline 58
Langford, Martin 86
launch 16, 80, 85
Learmount, David 21
lectures 37
life cycle 81
lifestyle magazines 14
Lord Chamberlain 79

Macintosh, Apple 36, 43
MacUser Awards 93
magazine 9, 10, 12, 14, 23, 32, 64, 68, 88, 92
mail 14, 26, 49, 67
mail order 67
mailing list 49, 56, 67
Management Consultancies Association 20
Management Today 92
marketing 12
Marketing 29, 94
media 9, 12, 14, 53, 54, 66, 94, 102, 107
media extravanganza 92
Media Guide, The 16, 55
media kit 62
media list 104
media monitoring 49, 56, 59
media relations basics 44–65
media tour 44, 52, 61, 62
media training 53, 81, 102
Media Week 93
Merrill Lynch 33, 42, 47, 80
message 10, 12, 13, 25, 31, 48, 53, 55, 76, 81, 82, 89
Mirror Group 15
model agency 77
Money Marketing 93
motivation 84
MS magazine 18
Museum of Natural History 88
Museum of the Moving Image 88
musician 78

National Investment Seminar Week 33
National Media Mind Competition 93
negative publicity 101
negatives 27
Newman, Cindy 80
news 21, 58
News International 15
newsclip 58
newsdesk 104
newsletter 67, 68
newspaper 9, 12, 14, 19, 21, 33, 62, 64, 76, 83, 104
newsreel 74
newsroom 104
NIMBY 84
no comment 101
Noel Gay Artists 77

101 Ways series 22, 25, 31, 47, 70, 71, 99
objectives, communications 11
objectives, marketing 11
objectives, publicity 10, 11, 17, 47
Official Secrets Act 22
Olympics 19, 42, 43, 55, 83, 86
opinion formers 12
optimist 28
organisations, professional 12
Oscars 92
outdoor poster 10

packaging 35
Parliament 21, 78
partnership 82
party 39, 87, 88
perception 35
performer 78
periodical 21
permission 57
personality 97
pessimist 28
PGA Tour of Europe 15, 38, 42
photo caption 45, 46, 49
photo opportunity 19, 40, 55, 57, 80, 84, 93
photocall 55
picture 45, 46, 49, 97
platform 70
plug 75
political reporter 21
politician 78, 99
positives 27
posters 9, 19, 37
PowerBook, Apple 36
PR Week 22, 29, 91, 92, 94
premium rate telephone 15, 64
presentation skills 52
presenter 54, 55
press agency 23, 104

Press Association 55
press clippings 33
press conference 16, 52, 54, 94, 102, 105
press kit 44, 55, 63, 64
press office 94
press release 23, 32, 44, 45, 47, 48, 59, 60
press release checklist 49
pressure group 100
print media 14
problem vs solution 28
product demonstration 54
production company, video 73, 90
professional organisations 12, 15, 47, 87
proof of purchase 37
proofreading 32, 49
public address system 54, 56
public relations 12, 54, 55
Public Relations Consultants Association 86
Public Relations Society of America 33
publication 21
publicity, basics 9–34
publicity, definition 9
publicity stunt 10
purchase, considered/impulse 35

quality dailies 15
quotes 48

race 41
radio 9, 10, 12, 21, 60, 62, 76, 90, 104, 105
radio clips 47, 60, 63
radio phone in 47
RAF Museum 85, 88
reality 35
recycling 35, 36, 37
reference manual 103, 106, 107
refreshments 54, 56
rehearsal 53, 55, 56
relevance 18, 31, 47, 57, 95, 97
reporting restrictions 22
reprint 45, 64
research 19, 26, 47, 49, 53

results 10, 33, 34, 56, 61, 68
reviewers 12, 44
risk assessment 102
Robberechts, Jan 69
Rodd, Michael 73
role model 80
Royal Patrons 79
royalty 8, 79
rumour 21, 99, 100
Russam, Charles 20

samples 45, 93
satellite 14, 58, 89, 92
scandal 99
scoop 23, 54
screening 17, 87, 88
script 55, 56
seminar 15, 22, 70, 82, 87, 88
shareholders 76
shelf life 48
showreel 73
signatures 84
Silver Anvil Award 33
sit-in 97
slant 28
slides 54, 56, 94
slogo 16, 42
smoking gun syndrome 100
sneak preview 39
solution vs problem 28
sound bite 10
sound system 56
source 9, 23, 26, 27, 68
special interests 76, 77, 84, 94
specialist 85
specification sheet 45
speech 14, 28, 33, 80
spokesperson 18, 47, 52, 53, 54, 61, 62, 63, 70, 80, 102, 103
sponsorship 10, 38, 39, 43, 78, 81, 91
sponsorship guarantees 39
sports 10, 21, 36, 38
stakeholder 75, 76, 83
statement 101, 102, 104, 105, 107
story angle planner 30
strategy 13, 17, 33, 55, 61, 92, 97, 102
stunt, publicity 10, 96–98

Sunday supplements 14
Sunday Times, The 20, 92
survey, research 20, 47
swipe footage 74
symposium 87

3M Company 40
tabloids 15, 99
talk show 62, 63
Telecom World 69
teleconference 89
telephone, freephone 76
telephone, premium rate 15, 64
telephone hot line 8
teletext 15
television 9, 10, 12, 14, 21, 22, 32, 35, 43, 72, 76, 104, 105
television network 53, 90
television news 21, 42, 102, 105
testing 25, 28
Thatcher, Margaret 55
third-party endorsement 16, 32, 52, 75, 78
Thomson Directory, The 66
Time 42, 64, 88
Times, The 19, 20, 29, 64
tracking 33
trade association 12, 21
trade development board 12
trade magazine 23, 29, 88, 104
trade show 15, 54, 87, 94
training 81
Training and Enterprise Council 13
transcripts 55

travel/tourist board 12
triggering events 45
TV 9, 10, 12, 14, 21, 22, 32, 35, 43, 72, 76, 104, 105
TV commercial 80, 92
TV station 97

update 28
users 12

value 33
venue 54, 88, 89
vertical publications 28
video 32, 33, 56, 60, 61, 70, 72, 82
video news release 44, 58, 59, 74
video production company 73, 90
video recorder 25
video wall 73
videocassettes 15
videotape 14, 53, 59
Visnews 59, 60, 74, 88
Voluntary Agencies Directory 78
vox pops, video 57, 60, 74, 82

Wall Street Journal Europe, The 46, 64
Watson, Stephen 89
Way a Day to Make It Pay, A 48
Whiplash, Miss 21
Whitehall 21
Wilson, Des 92
win/win situation 82

Yellow Pages 66, 77, 78
Your Guide to Antique Shopping in Britain 61, 70, 90